A CLEAR PATH

HOW TO MAKE MISSIONARY DISCIPLES IN YOUR PARISH

JIM JANSEN

Copyright © 2023 Jim Jansen.

A diligent effort has been made to find copyright holders and to obtain permission when needed. Please notify Anchor Consulting, LLC, at the address below if any copyright material appears to be improperly credited so corrections may be made for future printings.

All rights reserved. No part of this publication may be reproduced, distributed, or transmitted in any form or by any means, including photocopying, recording, or other electronic or mechanical methods, without the prior written permission of the publisher, except in the case of brief quotations embodied in critical reviews or certain other noncommercial uses permitted by copyright law. For permissions requests, write the publisher, addressed "Attention Permissions Coordinator," at the address below.

ISBN: 979-8-9887630-0-0
Library of Congress Control Number: 2023906222

Any references to historical events, real people, or real places used fictitiously. Names, characters, and places are products of the author's imagination.

Front cover image by Nicolas Fredrickson.

First printing edition 2023.
Anchor Consulting, LLC.
8510 S. 39th St.
Bellevue, NE 68147

Praise for
A Clear Path: How to Make Missionary Disciples in Your Parish

"Jim Jansen masterfully proposes a strategy for making missionary disciples in a typical Catholic parish. He calls it a clear path, and that path is rooted in his own experiences and successes working with real parishes in the Archdiocese of Omaha. It's well thought out, tested, and proven. And even includes all the very practical step-by-step tips for implementation. Every parish in the country should get a copy of this book!"

Jim Beckman
FOUNDER, IMPACTCENTER

"For over two decades, I witnessed the fruitfulness of Jim's outreach in making missionary disciples. The parish mission field is crucial to the Church's renewal in this Apostolic Age. I strongly recommend *A Clear Path* to anyone wanting to develop a plan to renew their parish!"

Curtis Martin
FOUNDER, FELLOWSHIP OF CATHOLIC UNIVERSITY STUDENTS (FOCUS)

"We were three-and-a-half years into transforming our parish and creating chaos before we realized we needed to make sense of what we were doing. People were losing steam, staff were getting frustrated, and key leaders were beginning to resent each other. We needed a clear path. I wish I had this book when we created our game plan. This book is a gift to every parish leader looking to make a disproportionate impact!"

Ron Huntley
PARISH RENEWAL SPECIALIST, HUNTLEY LEADERSHIP

"It is said that a vision without a plan is merely a dream. Jim Jansen has provided a tool which gives Catholic leaders a way to make a real plan for starting renewal in their parishes. Don't pass this book up. Read it. Study it. Use it."

Marcel LeJeune
PRESIDENT AND FOUNDER, CATHOLIC MISSIONARY DISCIPLES

"*A Clear Path* is a thoughtful, step-by-step guide for parishes to reimagine and refocus their mission toward fruitful discipleship. It answers a key question for parish evangelization: how do parishes that already have established systems and ministries develop new ways to form disciples within the parish? With a unified vision and 'a clear path!'"

Dr. Edward Sri
AUTHOR, *INTO HIS LIKENESS: BE TRANSFORMED AS A DISCIPLE OF CHRIST*

"I believe the Catholic Church in America stands on a precipice of tremendous impact. *A Clear Path* is just the type of book we need to scale this mountain. Jim walks leaders step-by-step into the necessary why and how for making a parish fruitful in forming deep disciples of Jesus. I love that he does this while simultaneously inspiring hope, vision, and continual reliance on the Holy Spirit."

Jason Simon
PRESIDENT, THE EVANGELICAL CATHOLIC

"If your parish has more programs and ministries than disciples, you need this book. *A Clear Path* outlines a step-by-step plan to grow and mature disciples in light of your parish realities. *A Clear Path* will challenge your parish to not only evangelize but strategize concrete ways to unleash the power of the Holy Spirit in making disciples. It reminds us that the Church doesn't have a mission, the mission has a Church."

Leyden Rovelo-Krull
DIRECTOR, OFFICE OF HISPANIC MINISTRY, DIOCESE OF KANSAS CITY-ST. JOSEPH

"Jim Jansen has offered an important perspective and contribution. He integrates practical wisdom with an awareness of the current challenges of the culture. That makes this new book a helpful resource for evangelizing those within our Catholic communities."

Msgr. James P. Shea
PRESIDENT, UNIVERSITY OF MARY

"With practical and accessible wisdom, Jim Jansen lays out a plan for making disciples in your parish that is steeped in real-world experience. Your parish's evangelization efforts will be blessed by taking this book's advice to heart."

Michael Hall
CATHOLIC CHRISTIAN OUTREACH CANADA, AUTHOR, *INTENTIONAL ACCOMPANIMENT: AN APPRENTICESHIP FOR A NEW GENERATION OF BUILDERS*

"True practitioners can make the best teachers, and Jim Jansen is one of the most experienced practitioners in the Church today. In *A Clear Path*, Jim helps parish leaders with an essential, but simple, idea: if you want your parish to make disciples, then you need to know how you do it! Jim will walk you from theological principles all the way through implementation to bear fruit that will last."

Tim Glemkowski
AUTHOR, *MADE FOR MISSION: RENEWING YOUR PARISH CULTURE*

Acknowledgements

From the very beginning it was clear the Lord was leading and guiding this project. My gratitude to him is expressed, in part, toward all those he gave me as helpers along the way.

I want to begin by thanking my wife, Kim, who is the professional writer in the family. I would also like to thank my editor, Elizabeth Wells, whose guidance was truly a providential gift. This project would not have come to completion without them.

I also want to thank my teammates and co-workers at the Archdiocese of Omaha. Your faithful labors in the trenches and countless hours in conversation with a whiteboard played an immeasurable role in shaping the articulation of the clear path concepts.

In a similar fashion, I am indebted to the work of so many faithful laborers in the vineyard, who have laid a foundation for these concepts and who have led the conversation on the New Evangelization here in North America. Of special note are Sherry Weddell, Tim Glemkowski, and Father James Mallon.

So, too, my personal experience in the world of campus ministry provided a foundational training in the missionary work of the Church. My introduction to missionary life with FOCUS (Fellowship of Catholic University Students) would not have happened without the invitation and patient mentorship of Dr. Ted Sri, Curtis Martin, and John Zimmer. Thanks for your investment in me as a leader. Special thanks to the work of The Evangelical Catholic and Catholic Christian Outreach of Canada.

I am grateful to Archbishop George Lucas and the pastors and parish staff who are laboring to make and mature disciples in their parishes and apostolates. This book is for you.

Contents

Foreword by Archbishop George Lucas 11
Introduction 13

Part I: What Is a Clear Path of Discipleship?
Chapter 1 Thresholds of Conversion and Discipleship 21
Chapter 2 The Benefits of a Clear Path 42
Chapter 3 A Path Fostering Conversion 51
Chapter 4 A Path Providing Clarity 64
Chapter 5 A Path Offering Connection 76

Part II: The Phases of Building a Clear Path
Introduction 91
Chapter 6 Phase 1: Assessment 93
Chapter 7 Phase 2: Discernment 106
Chapter 8 Phase 3: Implementation 116
Chapter 9 Phase 4: Communication 125
Chapter 10 Phase 5: Alignment 141
Chapter 11 Phase 6: Expansion 152

Part III: A Clear Path Case Study
Building St. Mary's "Highway to Heaven" 163

Conclusion 215

Appendix
I. Thresholds of Conversion and Discipleship 219
II. Steps on A Clear Path of Discipleship 220
III. Discernment Rosary Facilitator's Guide 221
IV. Discernment Rosary Sample Questions 223
V. Methods of Relational Prayer 224
VI. Clear Objectives, Facilitator's Guide 228
VII. Clear Objectives Worksheet 230
VIII. Planning Guide 231
IX. St. Mary's "Highway to Heaven" Image 232

Foreword

Several years ago, a series of listening sessions were held across the Archdiocese of Omaha. Participants were asked to share their hopes for the future of our parishes and archdiocese. Their input helped in the articulation of a pastoral vision for our local church.

Although expressed in a variety of ways, two things were heard repeatedly. First, Catholics desire a deeper and more lively relationship with Jesus. Second, they want to share their faith with family members and co-workers, but they don't know how.

Without realizing it, these ordinary parishioners are asking to be formed as disciples of Jesus Christ. They sense the Lord is offering them more and also asking something more of them. But they feel stuck in the same old ways of living, praying, and relating. They also see that the world is moving fast, sweeping people they care about along with it.

Formation in discipleship involves a realistic first step for someone who does not yet know the Lord, as well as a next step for one who has already experienced life in Christ. This lifelong journey cannot be strictly scripted, and the Holy Spirit will provide grace-filled surprises. At the same time, pastors and parish leaders will find it impossible to provide what parishioners deeply desire without offering a "clear path" on which disciples can experience growth in faith and in dedication to the mission of Christ.

Jim Jansen offers a practical guide for understanding the clear path and for building it in every parish. Where these efforts have begun in the Archdiocese of Omaha, we are already experiencing the fruit.

We are meant to be a pilgrim people. The clear path helps us move forward along the way the Lord has marked for us.

Most Reverend George J. Lucas
Archbishop of Omaha

Introduction

The odds are you know someone personally who has stopped practicing their faith. Maybe it's a co-worker or a neighbor. Maybe it is an old friend or someone from your own family. You are not alone.

The Church in the West is shrinking. For some of you, that is a shock. For others, it is old news. Whatever your reaction, it is a fact. Secularism, consumerism, and many other factors seem to be conspiring to rob the Church of her children and her place in society. Once-thriving faith communities of Europe, the United States, and Canada are experiencing rapid decline. Chances are your parish is feeling the effects.

Cultural commentators refer to it as a "change of the ages." For centuries, the Church dominated cultural, social, and political life in the West. Church historians call it the age of Christendom. It was a time when the culture reinforced the values of the gospel. It was beautiful, but it has rapidly come to an end.

We seem to be at the dawn of a new Apostolic Age. Similar to those years immediately following Jesus' death, resurrection, and ascension, when the apostles built the Church amidst extreme cultural opposition, today's Church must rediscover the heart of her purpose and the methods that continue spreading her message.

In this time of transition, it can feel like we are caught between two worlds. Many of the structures and modes of operation that once served us are no longer effective since they were designed for a different age. We find ourselves confused and overwhelmed by the effects of our people disengaging over the last few decades. Those remaining attempt to maintain operations with fewer and fewer resources. Already overstretched leaders are given increasing responsibilities. It feels like it is always the same people doing everything because it *is* the same people doing everything.

We cannot continue to operate in the same way. The good news is we are being called to something new…and old.

Missional Amnesia

For over 50 years, the Lord has been patiently and consistently calling the Church back to its missionary identity. It began with the Second Vatican Council, which called all Christians to holiness and mission. The Council said the Church was to be a light to the nations. Evangelization has always been the core of the Church's identity, but as this new Apostolic Age dawns, she must rediscover how to evangelize in the modern world.

The Church sometimes calls this process of rediscovering missionary identity "pastoral conversion." It is like an initial conversion in that it is a turning once again to the person of Jesus. The difference is what must be converted is not our attitudes about Jesus but our attitudes about our neighbor. We are being called to change the way we care for our people and our neighbors. At the heart of this change is making and maturing disciples in a culture that was once Christian but has now lost its way.

Making and maturing disciples in a hostile culture is really nothing new for the Church. Our history proves that we can and do thrive, even when the culture does not support our labors. The Church's founding in the Apostolic Age was in a culture similar to our own. The Church knows what it is to be missionary. Think of the countless saints like Patrick and Boniface who evangelized entire peoples and cultures. This is who we are.

Evangelization is a big word, and it can sometimes be intimidating. The thought of it makes many uncomfortable, but please hold your judgement. We will look at what evangelism really is and what it is not in Chapter 1. A lot has been written on evangelization lately, but the concept is not complex or new. Evangelization is all about making disciples. It is about introducing people to Jesus and helping them mature so they can fruitfully share their faith with others as missionary disciples. This is the urgent task of pastoral conversion – the rediscovery of making and maturing disciples.

In many ways, all the other challenges the Church faces today are just symptoms of this fundamental challenge to make disciples. Decreasing Mass attendance, shrinking financial giving, disregard for the poor, and the divisions of our society itself are all symptoms of one thing: the need to make and mature disciples.

A New Hope

There is hope. The Church is not experiencing decline everywhere. There are pockets of great renewal happening. Have you recently been to a college campus to witness the devotion of students filling a packed church for a 10 p.m. Mass on a Thursday evening? The Church is vibrant and alive if you know where to look.

Quietly and almost unseen, the Lord has also been at work renewing the Church through a series of groups referred to as ecclesial movements (ecclesial comes from the word "church" in Greek). Ecclesial movements are groups of disciples loyal to the Church, passionate in their expression of faith, but not necessarily formally connected to a parish community.

Ecclesial movements often have a special emphasis and unique way to live out the faith. The Church in Europe and South America has seen amazing things happen through these groups. Increasingly the Holy Spirit seems to be growing similar movements here in the United States and Canada. Movements like NET (National Evangelization Teams) Ministries, The Evangelical Catholic, St. Paul's Outreach, Jovenes para Cristo (Youth for Christ), FOCUS (The Fellowship of Catholic University Students), and others are experiencing explosive growth in their evangelization of young people. Adults are also experiencing this renewal through movements like Cursillo.

The rapid growth of these movements outside the confines of traditional parish life might cause us to wonder: Can parishes make disciples like movements do?

A Future for Parishes

Pope Francis addresses the question of mission and parish vitality in his encyclical, *The Joy of the Gospel*. He cites the flexibility and adaptivity of parishes as a reason for hope, and his hope is founded. The work of organizations that serve *within* parishes and apostolates that support parishes (e.g., Divine Renovation and Amazing Parish) are bearing fruit. There are a growing number of faith communities demonstrating that a parish can be dynamic, fruitful, and rediscover its missionary identity. Dozens around the country have already begun to do so.

In some ways, the aim of this book is to show that vibrancy and parish life are compatible. However, to revitalize our parishes, the parish community must rediscover its mission to make and mature disciples, and it must make a concrete plan to do so.

This book, and the clear path it covers, provides a concrete plan that addresses this rediscovery of mission and refocuses efforts to support this mission. Real parish renewal goes much deeper than our plans and structures. It is about culture and docility to the Holy Spirit.

A Clear Path does *not* focus on the specific skills and methods used to make disciples, such as leading a small group or sharing your faith story. There are many terrific books and conferences that can help teach those skills.

This book is about developing a plan for making disciples in your parish. It offers a framework so the missionary disciples who run the ministries of your parish flourish, regardless of the methods they use.

How to Use This Book

This book is written for pastors, parish leaders, and the everyday faithful who labor beside them on pastoral councils, evangelization committees, and in the countless volunteer ministries that make up our parishes. Although the concepts presented are deeply rooted in the history and pastoral practice of the Church, I have resisted theological and philosophical language. This book tries to make that timeless wisdom accessible to all.

This book is best read within a missional community, even if that community is small. Specifically, this book is designed to be utilized by pastors and parish leaders to spark conversation. There are discussion questions at the end of each chapter designed for that purpose. It can also be used by ministry leaders in a specific context like youth ministry to create a clear path for that ministry. You will find concrete advice with plenty of latitude to apply the concepts to the context of your parish and your ministry.

The book comes in three parts. Part I lays out the essential concepts behind a clear path of discipleship. Those concepts are foundational, and they will run throughout the book. Part II covers the phases for building a clear path of discipleship. It shares step-by-step instructions and proven wisdom for how to implement the concepts from Part I. In Part III, you will read a fictional case study of St. Mary's Parish and their efforts to build a clear path.

The fictional case study is meant to provide inspiration and imagination for how the journey might unfold for your parish or ministry. Any resemblance to particular individuals is coincidental. The characters in the case study are a combination of dozens of real people and real stories designed to paint a picture of what the journey looks like in practice.

This book can be read in a few days, but it will take months to digest and potentially years to implement. The full fruition of a clear path of discipleship will likely take many years with ups, downs, twists, and turns. Some of those turns will lead to dead ends, and others will lead to the joyful and unexpected fruit of changed lives. The journey's length and rigor require a firm conviction to persevere in the task. I hope the understanding and conversations sparked by this book will give you the wisdom and conviction necessary to build a clear path of discipleship.

Part I
What Is a Clear Path of Discipleship?

Chapter 1
The Thresholds of Conversion and Discipleship

For the last 50 years, much of the Church has been slowly rediscovering her missionary identity. In 1975, Pope Saint Paul VI began to call the Church back to her missionary identity by reminding us the Church exists to evangelize. He said:
"*'We wish to confirm once more that the task of evangelizing all people constitutes the essential mission of the Church.' It is a task and mission which the vast and profound changes of present-day society make all the more urgent. Evangelizing is in fact the grace and vocation proper to the Church, her deepest identity. She exists in order to evangelize....*"[1]

The Church is a big organization. We do a lot of stuff. Think of the countless food pantries, counseling centers, hospitals, and educational efforts accomplished through the Catholic Church around the world. In every corner of the globe, we are busy attending to the needs of our neighbors. And yet, if Pope Saint Paul VI is correct, and I think he is, all of the Church's activity is somehow at the service of her essential mission of evangelization.

This is where some of you start to hold your breath. For some of us, the word evangelization conjures up images of street corners and going door to door. These ideas make some of us uncomfortable. Do not worry. You can relax. Part of the reason you might feel uncomfortable is that these methods of evangelization do not suit you. A fuller understanding of evangelization will help you find your place in the mission in

---

[1] Pope Paul VI, *Evangelization in the Modern World*, 1975, #14. © Dicastero per la Comunicazione-Libreria Editrice Vaticana. He begins by quoting the *"Declaration of the Synod Fathers"* (October 1974) and then expounds further by adding his own emphasis.

a way that suits you and your parish because it will fit the natural sharing of the gifts God has given you.

If evangelization is the essential mission of the universal Church, it is also the essential mission of our parishes and all of us who are baptized. When we have a full picture of what evangelization is, it is much easier to see how the Lord is calling us to take part in a way that fits with how he uniquely made each of us. We all have a part to play in inviting others to take the next step in his or her journey of faith.

At the risk of oversimplifying just to make you feel more comfortable, let me suggest a basic definition. *Evangelization is the making of disciples.* Pope Saint Paul VI explains evangelization much in the same way as he continues his meditation on the role of evangelization in the mission of the Church.[2] He goes on to say that evangelization is a process, punctuated by key moments. That process results in an individual being "renewed spiritually through a personal encounter and lived communion with Jesus Christ."[3] This process of evangelization is all about the changing of lives with the Good News of Jesus Christ.

I will expand on the process of evangelization in just a bit. For now, I want to highlight the gift of Pope Saint Paul VI's teaching on the mission of the Church to make disciples. The reminder that the Church exists to evangelize could not have come at a better time. At first glance, the providential timing may not be clear. At the time of Pope Saint Paul VI, seminaries were full and Mass attendance was high. In a little more than a generation, the culture that supported the faith has almost completely disappeared. Evangelization is fundamental

---

[2] Pope Paul VI, *Evangelization in the Modern World*, 1975, #7-17. © Dicastero per la Comunicazione-Libreria Editrice Vaticana.

[3] *The New Evangelization for the Transmission of the Christian Faith*, Lineamenta for the Synod of Bishops' XIII Ordinary General Assembly, February 2011, #22. © Dicastero per la Comunicazione-Libreria Editrice Vaticana.

patterns. It is a process punctuated by key moments of growth, which we will call "thresholds."[5]

Over the centuries, the Church has articulated this process in a variety of ways. Theologians and spiritual writers have used technical language to speak about the Lord's mysterious work to draw people back to himself. Collectively, the Church calls this the catechumenal model. It includes technical words like adherence, initiatory catechesis, mystagogy, kerygma, and proclamation. One of the most recent articulations comes from Pope Benedict XVI where he articulates the process of forming missionary disciples as encounter, conversion, discipleship, communion, and mission.[6] All of these words describe key moments in the process of conversion and growth in discipleship.

More recently, however, efforts by authors, such as Sherry Weddell, Tim Glemkowski, Curtis Martin, and countless others, have begun to express the Church's timeless teaching about evangelization in ordinary everyday language. FOCUS articulates it as "Win, Build, Send."[7] Sherry Weddell introduced the "thresholds of conversion" into a Catholic context. The Church's language for evangelization is becoming more accessible.

What follows is a simple synthesis of several expressions of the process of evangelization. It will provide a foundation for understanding the process of conversion, the moment of decision, and growth in discipleship – all critical components of the process of evangelization. Together they form a foundation for building a clear path of discipleship in a parish.

---

[5] Excerpts from *Forming Intentional Disciples* © Sherry Weddell, 2012. Published by OSV. Used by permission.

[6] Pope Benedict XVI, Aparecida Document, Letter to the Bishops of Latin America and the Caribbean, 2007, #278. © Dicastero per la Comunicazione-Libreria Editrice Vaticana.

[7] *Win, Build, Send* framework used by permission of Fellowship of Catholic University Students.

DISCLAIMER: *Conversion is a very personal journey.* Although the Church has recognized patterns for how the Lord leads through conversion and growth as a disciple, an individual person's journey may not seem to fit into neat categories. Evangelization is a mysterious work of grace. The Church has articulated a process, but in reality, it is often two steps forward and one step back. Even the best mental framework must be held lightly as we consider how to support an individual soul's particular journey.

The Holy Spirit is the secret power behind all our efforts to build a clear path and to accompany individuals on their personal journey of faith. Ultimately, it is our attentiveness to him and his work that makes all the difference. You will want to keep the work of the Spirit in mind as we go through the thresholds of conversion and discipleship. Even when we cannot see his work directly, he is the one behind the scenes orchestrating everything for the glory of the Father and the salvation of souls.

Thresholds of Conversion

The process of conversion is how someone moves from distrust to a firm decision in faith to trust Christ as their Savior. Conversion is marked by several key moments or thresholds. These thresholds are generally intuitive, but they provide a helpful framework for understanding the sometimes-subtle work of the Lord in our lives.

On subsequent pages, you will see images of the Thresholds of Conversion and Discipleship. For a complete visual image, see Appendix I.

These threshold images were developed by the Parish Support Team from the Archdiocese of Omaha. I am particularly grateful to Andy Dejka who helped bring these ideas to life as tools for training parish leaders. These images build on the work of FOCUS[8], Sherry Weddell and Tim Glemkowski. These images, which use the idea that the thresholds of conversion are similar to planting seeds and watching them grow, are used with permission from the Archdiocese of Omaha.

Conversion Thresholds

Trust

A person has a positive association with Jesus or an individual Catholic and may begin asking questions out of passive curiosity.

Openness

A person admits to a general need or desire for personal spiritual change. This is not the same as a commitment to specific changes.

Seeking

A person moves from being passive to actively seeking to know the God who is calling him or her. The seeker is engaged in a spiritual quest.

Decision

The decision, in faith, to follow Jesus as an obedient disciple in the midst of the Church, which brings about new life.

The first and foundational threshold of conversion is trust, where someone has a positive association with Jesus or the Church. Unfortunately, in an increasingly post-Christian society, trust cannot be assumed. If we are attentive to the fears and concerns of those around us, we must admit that Christians, the Church, and even the person of Christ are often

---

[8] Graphic adapted from *Discipleship Roadmap* framework by permission of Fellowship of Catholic University Students.

viewed with suspicion. In other words, the default setting of many of our friends, neighbors, co-workers, and family members is often distrust.

Pre-Trust – Sometimes pre-trust is simply a lack of exposure to Christians or the person of Christ. Sometimes it is deep-seated suspicion and the result of hurtful personal experiences. Regardless of the cause, the effect is the same. For individuals who are in a state of pre-trust, an appeal to authority, tradition, and institutional credibility falls on deaf ears. Where there is no trust, it must be built.

Trust is built by...wait for it...being trustworthy. Trust is built by being kind, honest, selfless, and attentive to the concerns of others. Building trust may take many years. It involves friendship but not just a friendship that comes easily due to common interest. It is built from patient and often sacrificial love.

Sometimes we may seem to have little in common with those with whom we are called to build trust. This should not be surprising. After all, the center of our lives as a disciple is not something that this other person shares or even finds attractive – at least at first.

Relationships built through patient love and friendship provide a foundation for the first threshold in the process of conversion.

Trust – A person at the threshold of trust has a positive association with Jesus or an individual Catholic. They may begin asking questions out of passive curiosity. They may also have one or several areas of mistrust that remain.

As you can imagine, individuals at this threshold are often not interested in your parish's programming. If there is a connection to the parish, it is probably relational rather than institutional or communal. Sincere and authentic friendship is the primary means by which these individuals can be drawn closer to Christ and the local parish community. This friendship and trust are the necessary prerequisites for making meaningful invitations.

It is worth noting that someone may claim to be Catholic and have received the sacraments of initiation yet remain socially and spiritually apart from Christ and the community of faith. We will discuss this phenomenon more later, but for now, I encourage you to ask about people's stories and lived experiences – not simply if they were baptized or grew up going to church.

WARNING: *Even after you have labored to establish a foundation of friendship and trust, your invitations may still be met with rejection.* That is okay. Be patient and persevere in authentic friendship. If you have no agenda other than love, I promise your efforts will bear fruit even if you don't personally get to see the results.

Openness – A person at the threshold of openness admits to a general need or desire for personal spiritual change. This is different from a commitment to specific changes. The movement from the threshold of trust to the threshold of openness is often precipitated by a significant life event, which awakens the individual to their unmet spiritual needs. Events like the loss of a job, the death of a spouse, divorce, or financial difficulties often spark this awareness.

It is important to note, however, that *admitting the need for change is not the same thing as a specific commitment to change.* Just because someone realizes they need to get in shape does not mean they have committed to a workout routine. You can recognize openness by a person's sincere willingness to admit something is missing in their life. Again, authentic friendship and relationships make all the difference in helping individuals transition from openness to the next threshold of seeking.

Seeking – A person at the threshold of seeking moves from being passive in their spiritual journey to actively seeking to know the God who is calling him or her. The seeker is engaged in a spiritual quest. This threshold is marked by a sincere and persistent desire to know and find answers to questions that have now become *personal*.

Individuals who are seeking are often eager to learn. You might find them reading spirituality and self-help books from a variety of faith traditions. Their learning differs from those who have already decided to follow Christ as a disciple. Seekers are still weighing their options. They are still sifting and evaluating, even if they are frequently present within the Christian community. They may have a considerable number of friends who live as disciples. They may even consider themselves to be a part of a parish community, even if they have not personally made a firm decision to follow Christ.

This might be a surprising idea. Can someone be a part of a parish and not have decided to follow Christ? Yes, and in fact, this may be more common than we realize. Pope Saint John Paul II noted this phenomenon back in 1979. He said that even among those who approach the parish for faith formation, "initial evangelization has often not taken place... [they are] still without any explicit personal attachment to Jesus Christ."[9]

That is why an explicit decision to follow Jesus Christ is so pivotal in the process of evangelization. We should never assume that someone has made a personal and explicit decision to follow Jesus.

Decision – A person at the threshold of decision is wrestling with the commitment to follow Jesus as an obedient disciple within the Church. It is both a commitment to follow the person of Jesus and a commitment to engage with the local community of disciples. It is the essential moment of encounter and conversion in the lives of those who call themselves disciples. Pope Benedict XVI said it this way: "Faith thus takes shape as an encounter with a person to whom we entrust our

---

[9] Pope John Paul II, *Catechesis in Our Time* 1979, #19. © Dicastero per la Comunicazione-Libreria Editrice Vaticana.

whole life."[10] Although not everyone's story will have a dramatic moment of encounter and conversion, every true disciple must make a decision in faith to entrust themselves to Jesus.

Decision

The decision, in faith, to follow Jesus as an obedient disciple in the midst of the Church, which brings about new life.

Those at the threshold of decision *need* a clear proclamation of the core message of the gospel and an invitation to entrust themselves to Jesus. Pope Saint John Paul II referred to the proclamation in this moment as the *hinge* on which all evangelization turns.[11] All our efforts at evangelization lead up to this moment, and all we do to help others grow and mature flows from it.

This proclamation of the gospel really is the essential moment of evangelization. Pope Saint Paul VI said it this way: "Evangelization will always contain... a clear proclamation that, in Jesus Christ... salvation is offered to all men, as a gift of God's grace and mercy."[12]

Individuals who are at the threshold of decision are recognizable by their weighing the claims of Jesus. They appreciate evidence and explanation for Jesus' claims. They often appreciate a personal call to conversion. Although the

---

[10] Pope Benedict XVI, *The Word of the Lord*, 2010, #25. © Dicastero per la Comunicazione-Libreria Editrice Vaticana.

[11] Pope John Paul II, *Mission of the Redeemer* (#44 emphasis added). © Dicastero per la Comunicazione-Libreria Editrice Vaticana.

[12] Pope Paul VI, *Evangelization in the Modern World*, 1975, #27. © Dicastero per la Comunicazione-Libreria Editrice Vaticana.

specificity and directness of that call would have been off putting and unhelpful for someone at the very beginning of the process of conversion, it is now essential to their continued growth.

The Four "Rs" of the Core Gospel Message

It is worth taking some time to examine the core message of the gospel that forms the heart of this proclamation. Although the gospel can be articulated a thousand different ways, there are generally four main points which must be clearly expressed.

Relationship: God loves us and made us for relationship with him and others (Jn. 3:16).

Ruin: Sin ruins our relationship and isolates us now and for eternity (Rom. 6:23).

Restore: Jesus restores our relationship with God by his death and resurrection (Rom. 5:8).

Response: Our response to accept Jesus opens us to life eternal (Rev. 3:20).

These four points are a summary of the core message of the gospel. This core message is often called the kerygma. "Kerygma" is just the Greek word for proclamation. Over time it has come to refer to the core message of the gospel that is proclaimed.

Entire chapters, and even entire books, have been written on the proclamation of the gospel. From my experience, the Church in the United States is just beginning to rediscover the power of this proclamation for evangelization. My own embrace of this practice made all the difference in my life as a missionary. Embracing proclamation as the hinge moment of evangelization is truly a game changer for parishes and ministries.

For now, it is enough to remind ourselves that every individual must make a decision for or against the person of Jesus. This goes much deeper than our religious upbringing or whether we happen to be registered as part of a faith community. We must decide in faith to trust Jesus with our lives. In fact, we must make this decision every day.

Jesus is either who he says he is, or he is not. He has already given himself to us completely on the Cross. He gave himself to us before we were aware of his love or able to respond. He asks us for the reciprocal gift of ourselves to him. A careful reading of the gospels reveals that Jesus does not let people walk the fence. He asks people to decide who he is. He tells us we cannot serve two masters and that we must take up our cross and follow him (Mt. 16:15, Mt. 6:24, Mt. 16:24). Jesus unequivocally and unapologetically asks for our complete trust. He calls people to decision, and so should we.

From my experience, the threshold of decision and the moment of proclamation are the most dynamic and exciting parts of the process of evangelization. Pope Benedict XVI said it this way: "Without the *kerygma*, the other aspects of this process are condemned to sterility, with hearts not truly converted to the Lord."[13]

Remember what makes proclamation and the threshold of decision a dynamic reality is free will. People can and do say "no" to the gospel. We must always respect people's free will and maintain hope knowing that a "no" today is not necessarily a "no" forever. The most dramatic stories of conversion come from those who made a decision for Christ only after many patient and repeated invitations.

A person who has made this decision for Christ can now rightly be called a disciple, and this decision releases grace which changes everything.

Thresholds of Discipleship

Beginning Disciple – A person at this threshold has committed to following Jesus by turning away from sin. They are willing to make sacrifices to personally grow. They strive

---

[13] Pope Benedict XVI, Aparecida Document, Letter to the Bishops of Latin America and the Caribbean, 2007, #278. © Dicastero per la Comunicazione-Libreria Editrice Vaticana.

to live the principles of Christian life. Individuals at this threshold are hungry to learn but no longer for the sake of weighing a decision for Christ and the Church. They are now convinced that Jesus and his Church have the words of eternal life.

Beginning disciples are easily recognized by their eagerness to know, understand, and embrace the teachings of Jesus. They are beginning to live as disciples. Sin will inevitably remain a part of their lives, but they are eager, with the help of his grace, to turn away from sin.

Individuals at this threshold need both instruction and models of discipleship. They desire to know the teachings of the Church and to live like Christ. Explicit instruction must be accompanied by people who are living examples and who have a similar vocation and state in life. This reinforcement of living examples within the parish community is invaluable to beginning disciples.

Among the parish community's first tasks is to teach beginning disciples how to pray. Their decision to follow Jesus was likely sparked by a moment of encounter. That encounter must be nourished and deepened with habits of personal prayer. Beginning disciples especially need instruction on *relational prayer* that keeps them connected to the person of Jesus and fuels their ongoing conversion.

Relational prayer is simply personal and conversational prayer with the Lord as one friend might speak to another and deepens the relationship between ourselves and the God who created and loves us. The methods of relational prayer include the liturgy (Mass) and devotions (Rosary), but they are founded on the Church's ancient methods of personal prayer. Personal prayer practices include Lectio Divina and other methods of prayer which are designed to spark a conversation with the Lord. (See Appendix V.)

Habits of prayer connect people to the Lord who does the heavy lifting of forming them as his disciples. Relational prayer becomes a primary place where the love of God grows.

As this habit of prayer grows, it will eventually overflow to others as a disciple begins to become missionary.

Discipleship Thresholds

Beginning Disciple

A person has committed to following Jesus by turning away from sin, and makes any sacrifice in order to personally grow, and lives habits of the Christian life.

Missionary Disciple

A person has decided to personally answer the call to take part in the mission of the Church by sharing the Good News.

Fruitful Disciple

A person is fully equipped for lifelong Catholic mission and makes any sacrifice to help another person to grow spiritually.

Missionary Disciple – A person who has reached the threshold of becoming a missionary disciple has decided to personally answer the call to take part in the mission of Jesus by sharing the Good News. This person is not only aware of the call to share their faith, but they have made a firm decision to share Christ with others, even if the expression of how they will participate remains unclear to them.

Missionary disciples can be recognized, in part, by their sense of calling. Regardless of the particulars of who and how they serve, they do so out of a sense of calling from the Lord.

Missionary disciples know the Lord is sending them, and they want to go.

Individuals at this threshold need to be equipped for their personal mission to share the Good News. The ways an individual may participate in this mission are as varied as the individuals themselves. They need help discerning where God has called them and how he has made *them* to share the Good News. This may look like being a patient and kind neighbor whose wordless witness establishes a bridge of trust. It could also look like a joy-filled teacher or ministry leader within the parish community. It may also be a particular calling to the corporal works of mercy which build trust and open hearts for the message of the gospel. Individualized mentorship and assessments designed to help people discover how they have been gifted for mission can be invaluable for assisting individuals at this threshold. Examples of assessments are Gallup StrengthsFinder (now CliftonStrengths®) and Catherine of Siena Institute's Called and Gifted ™ Discernment Process.

Regardless of the form their personal mission will take, individuals at the threshold of missionary disciple need to be taught simple methods of intercessory prayer. Intercessory prayer is the practice of beseeching the Lord for others. It is personal like relational prayer, but rather than a conversation centered on our own needs, it expands to our concern for others. In our intercessory prayer for others, the Lord begins to show us his love for others. Even more, he fills us with that love. Intercessory prayer becomes a place where the love of neighbor grows.

Fruitful Disciple – A person who has entered the threshold of being a fruitful disciple has embraced the call to mission and their efforts have borne fruit. They gladly make any sacrifice to help another person grow spiritually. This person is not only aware of and equipped to take part in the Church's mission of sharing the Good News, but they have done so in a fruitful way. Regardless of whether their labors have been simple or extraordinary, they have borne fruit in the changed lives of others.

Individuals at this threshold need the ongoing support of a community of other missionary disciples. They need ongoing formation and a team of individuals who share a similar mission. Jesus always sent his disciples out two by two because he knew the challenges disciples face on mission. *Being on mission is a team sport.*

Fruitful disciples need to collaborate with a wider community of disciples, who complement their gifting. For example, if a missionary disciple is gifted at building trust, another disciple gifted as a teacher could be helpful in assisting their efforts to accompany people who are eager to learn about the faith. Together, these disciples can do what they could not do individually.

Collaboration is one of the keys to recognizing fruitful disciples. They will seek out friendships with and assistance from other fruitful disciples. They are passionate about helping people through the process of conversion and discipleship. They have seen the Lord work through their labors, and it is one of the greatest joys of their life.

Finally, the prayer of fruitful disciples is, well, fruitful. It is the secret power behind all their service. Prayer is a deeply ingrained daily habit for fruitful disciples. They need guidance regarding prayer, drawn from the classic spiritual traditions of the Church.

How to "Meet Them Where They Are...."

If there is one catch phrase for evangelization that most people know, it is this: "You have to meet people where they are...." The phrase is true, but for many of us, the challenge is not that we are unwilling to meet people where they are in the journey. The challenge is *recognizing* where they are in the journey.

I must admit my own attempts to support individuals in their journeys were not always fruitful. Often, my efforts fell flat because I was not aware or attentive to where people were in the process of conversion and discipleship. I cannot tell you how many times I gave great Catholic books to people who did not exhibit openness and were therefore not interested. I tried to rally people to share their faith before they had really decided for Jesus. Mostly, my mistakes were innocent and the product of genuine care without awareness of the process of conversion and discipleship.

When I learned the process and began to share my faith with an awareness of it, I was much more fruitful. When a whole parish community begins to attend to the process of conversion and discipleship, lives really begin to change. It is attentiveness to the process of evangelization that truly allows us to "meet people where they are."

One of the best ways to do this is to prayerfully reflect on the person and what their needs may be. Prayerfully discerning who we should approach, asking good questions, and listening deeply is integral to effectively helping individuals move through the thresholds. When we begin with prayer, we can feel more confident that we are following God's plan, not only for us but for the person with whom we feel called to accompany. Check out Appendices III and IV on the Discernment Rosary and Appendix V on Relational Prayer for simple ideas to bring prayer and discernment deeper into your efforts to accompany others on their journey.

As we close this chapter, I cannot emphasize enough how important understanding the process of evangelization is to making disciples in a parish. Parishes that recognize their call to make disciples but still lack a clear understanding of the thresholds of conversion will struggle to connect with individuals at the start of their faith journey. Parishes that lack awareness of the thresholds of discipleship will be unable to effectively facilitate growth of disciples toward full maturity in Christ.

Only mature missionary disciples consistently impact and change lives. Mature missionary disciples are key to serving individuals at every threshold, especially at the conversion thresholds. Only mature disciples can embody the love of Jesus the Good Shepherd who leaves the 99 in pursuit of the one lost sheep.

In the next chapter, we will begin to look at the benefits and the key elements that make a clear path an effective framework for making and maturing disciples.

Thresholds of Conversion and Discipleship

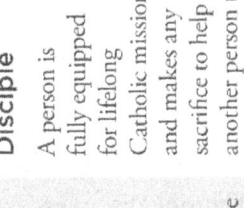

Trust
A person has a positive association with Jesus or an individual Catholic and may begin asking questions out of passive curiosity.

Openness
A person admits to a general need or desire for personal spiritual change. This is not the same as a commitment to specific changes.

Seeking
A person moves from being passive to actively seeking to know the God who is calling him or her. The seeker is engaged in a spiritual quest.

Decision
The decision, in faith, to follow Jesus as an obedient disciple in the midst of the Church, which brings about new life.

Beginning Disciple
A person has committed to following Jesus by turning away from sin, and makes any sacrifice in order to personally grow, and lives habits of the Christian life.

Missionary Disciple
A person has decided to personally answer the call to take part in the mission of the Church by sharing the Good News.

Fruitful Disciple
A person is fully equipped for lifelong Catholic mission and makes any sacrifice to help another person to grow spiritually.

Questions for Reflection

1. What stirs in your heart and mind as you hear recent popes call the Church to evangelization and making disciples?
2. What are the thresholds people pass through in the process of conversion?
3. Where have you heard an explicit proclamation of the gospel recently?
4. Where have you seen the thresholds of conversion and discipleship unfolding in someone's life? In your own life?
5. What might an awareness of the process of conversion and discipleship do for your parish?
6. What might be the consequences of a parish or ministry not understanding the thresholds of conversion?
7. What might be the consequences of a parish or ministry not understanding the thresholds of discipleship?

Chapter 2
The Benefits of a Clear Path

At the close of the last chapter, I said that a clear path provides a framework for a parish's mission to make disciples. That is the good news. The bad news is that establishing a clear path framework is going to take time and energy. You will have to say "no" to good things to make better things happen. You will encounter confusion and resistance. It will not happen overnight. I estimate that it could take three to five years to build a fully functioning clear path. For most parishes, that is a significant investment of time and energy. I want you to know it is worth the effort.

Let me offer two items for your encouragement as we begin: a quote from Pope Francis and a few benefits you can expect from building a clear path.

As you read this quote, please note how Pope Francis compares the transformation of the Church's structures to a type of conversion. He calls it, "pastoral conversion." Our efforts to change the way we do things will feel a bit like this conversion.

Okay, here is Pope Francis.

"I dream of... a missionary impulse capable of transforming everything, so that the Church's customs, ways of doing things, times and schedules, language and structures can be suitably channeled for the evangelization of today's world rather than for her self-preservation. The renewal of structures demanded by pastoral conversion can only be understood in this light: as part of an effort to make them more mission-oriented...."[14]

A clear path of discipleship is a concrete way to bring what Pope Francis calls the "missionary impulse" to life. The

---

[14] Pope Francis, *Joy of the Gospel*, 2013, #27. © Dicastero per la Comunicazione-Libreria Editrice Vaticana.

transformation is a work of grace, and it goes much deeper than simply restructuring a few programs. Pope Francis knows that pastoral conversion requires a change in our hearts and minds away from self-preservation toward the evangelization of friends, family, and neighbors who do not know Christ. We must channel our customs and ways of doing things toward making disciples. A clear path of discipleship does just that. A clear path helps you live Pope Francis' "missionary impulse" for the evangelization of today's world…or at least your corner of it.

The Benefits of a Clear Path of Discipleship

Here is your second bit of encouragement. As you begin the process of building a clear path, the following benefits begin immediately, and they continue to grow and multiply as all the pieces come together.

A clear path makes disciples within our parishes.

So much of what afflicts parishes today is the lack of intentional disciples within our congregations. Even among those regularly attending Mass, a shockingly low percentage seem to be intentionally living as committed disciples of Jesus.[15] We spend time addressing the symptoms of the problem by trying to encourage people to act like disciples. Consider financial giving and community service, for example. We try announcements, then encouragement, and then low-grade extortion in the form of "required" service hours. Consider civic involvement. We urge people to vote with a Catholic conscience. We challenge people to be a light in the larger community, yet the influence of faith continues to diminish in our culture. Consider evangelization. We tell people to share their faith. We ask them to share their faith with children, family, friends, and neighbors, but our congregations continue to shrink.

---

[15] Excerpts from *Forming Intentional Disciples* © Sherry Weddell, 2012. Published by OSV. Used by permission.

All of this encouragement is good, but it is ignored by those who are not intentional disciples. Intentional disciples already want to live like disciples. They may still need encouragement, but the fundamental disposition is already there.

A clear path of discipleship gives your parish a way to make disciples within your parish. Becoming a disciple is a life-changing experience, especially for those who have been a part of a Christian community for many years but have never quite fully decided for Christ. Imagine the power if more of your parishioners were to experience the life, hope, peace, and joy of a life of discipleship. When they do, what was once sterile comes to life.

A clear path connects non-believers with your parish.

A clear path allows your parish to meet non-believers where they are in their faith journey. It enables your parish to fruitfully engage with those who are apathetic, atheists, spiritual seekers, fallen away Catholics, and anyone else you might encounter. It provides a spiritual on-ramp for everyone, no matter where they are in their spiritual journey. We often talk about the need to meet people where they are. A clear path of discipleship helps your parish do exactly that.

New people coming into your parish add life and vitality, especially when they are experiencing the power of the gospel for the first time. There is something special about the excitement new members bring that helps remind everyone of the gift of faith. Imagine what dozens of new disciples would do to revitalize your parish.

A clear path helps people take ownership of their spiritual growth.

We can easily feel overwhelmed by the number of options for participation in our parishes. People do not need any help being busy. Sometimes when people join a parish, they receive a giant parish ministry guidebook with a list of dozens of ministries. Although well meaning, so many choices paralyze people, preventing them from taking action. You have probably experienced this kind of "choice paralysis" flipping through the endless movie options online. It is hard to decide with so many options. People wonder, "What is the right next step for me?" It may be counterintuitive, but narrowing the options with a clear path gives people greater freedom to act.

People who want to grow need a few clearly designated next steps to take ownership of their journey. Imagine how people who take ownership of their spiritual growth would change your parish culture. When people know their next steps, they can show initiative rather than acting like passive and demanding customers. A clear path helps everyone know and own their next step on the journey.

A clear path matures disciples.

Mature disciples not only function as disciples by serving and sharing their faith, but they do so with wisdom and the power of the Holy Spirit. There is no substitute for mature, well-formed leaders, who have been equipped for evangelization. Imagine a pastoral council that combines a love for the parish, experience in professional life, *and* the gift of wise supernatural counsel. Imagine disciples who serve with discernment flowing from the fruit of prayer. That kind of counsel and discernment only comes from mature disciples, and that maturity must be cultivated. A clear path matures disciples in prayer and equips them for fruitful evangelization. The Synod of Bishops in 2011 wrote it this way: "People are able to evangelize only when they have been evangelized...renewed spiritually through a personal encounter and lived communion with Jesus Christ."[16] Many disciples are hungering for formation in evangelization. A commitment to provide support for growth and maturity will draw disciples hungry for more to your parish community.

---

[16] *The New Evangelization for the Transmission of the Christian Faith*, Lineamenta for the Synod of Bishops' XIII Ordinary General Assembly, February 2011, #22. © Dicastero per la Comunicazione-Libreria Editrice Vaticana.

A clear path fosters true collaboration.

Evangelization is a team sport. The Spirit gives many different gifts and talents. Imagine all the gifts and charisms of the Spirit working in harmony to make disciples. It is like a sports team with everyone in his or her right position. Each ministry and every person will play a distinct role in that process. When a parish has articulated a clear path of discipleship, all ministries can unify around the common mission of making disciples. With a clear path, they can all consciously and cooperatively work for the same goal. For example, people with the charisms of mercy and healing would play a key role in connecting with non-believers. Once they have built relationships with non-believers, they can introduce them to disciples with the charism of evangelization. These disciples would assist with the parish's efforts to foster encounter and conversion.

Once people have responded to the gospel and become disciples, they need formation to live as disciples. At that point, they would benefit from people with the charisms of teaching and pastoring. Once those disciples are ready to personally answer the call to mission, they need mature disciples with charisms of encouragement and wisdom to help equip and launch them into their personal mission as missionary disciples.

One of the greatest obstacles to evangelization today is that even those who recognize evangelization as an essential mission of the Church often think it is someone else's job. Now there are many reasons people do not take personal responsibility for evangelization, but I believe one of the main reasons is an overly narrow concept of evangelization. A clear path provides a full and broad concept of evangelization. With the full process of evangelization in mind, everyone can find a role that fits them and their unique gifts. Just like a good football team, your parish team has room for linemen, receivers, quarterbacks, and yes, even kickers.

A clear path focuses parish resources on fruitfulness.

Sometimes it can feel like resources are scarce. Sometimes they really are scarce. If we are going to bear the fruit of changed lives, we must invest our time, energy, and resources in activities that are focused on the mission of making disciples. Some ministries have an intrinsically greater potential to bear spiritual fruit than others. For example, ministries that explicitly proclaim the basic gospel message and personally accompany the participants often bear more fruit. When a parish prioritizes ministries that have the greatest potential for making and maturing disciples, fruitfulness naturally follows. A clear path helps parishes align whatever resources are available to the making and maturing of disciples.

A clear path keeps people from getting lost.

Our spiritual journey can be long, winding, and sometimes lonely. There is no denying that, despite our best efforts, people often get lost along the way. The increasing size of parishes, the distractions of our culture, and the modern pace of life make it more difficult to shepherd people through their personal faith journey.

A clear path helps a pastor and parish leaders shepherd people through the conversion process and growth as a disciple. A clear path provides a simple connected pathway that removes some of the confusion and difficulty people experience as they try to grow and mature in their spiritual journey. More than just programs and ministries, a clear path provides living "connectors," people who can help others move and grow in your faith community.

The Three Elements of a Clear Path

So, now we are ready to dive into the power of a clear path of discipleship to help a parish become a missional community focused on making disciples. If the mission of the Church is indeed to make disciples, then a clear path of discipleship is the concrete expression of that mission in your parish. A parish community must have clarity about how they make disciples. Let us return to our simple definition:

A clear path of discipleship is a simple, step-by-step plan for making and maturing disciples by the power of the Holy Spirit.

In its essence, a clear path is a strategy for making disciples. It prioritizes and coordinates the efforts of existing disciples in a parish toward the mission to make and mature disciples.

There are three key elements that make a clear path an effective strategy to make and mature disciples.

Conversion – A clear path fosters conversion by providing a framework with steps for growth through the thresholds.

Clarity – A clear path provides clarity by highlighting a few ministries for simplicity and maximum fruitfulness.

Connection – A clear path offers connection between highlighted ministries, so no one gets lost on the journey.

DISCLAIMER: *Although a clear path will always have these elements, no two parishes are the same, and no two parishes will end up with the exact same clear path.* The framework will be similar, but the details will be different depending on the gifts of the community and needs of the mission field.

A parish in a university town, for example, will serve a very different population than one that serves a small rural community. They will likely have quite different clear paths. So too, the path of a parish located in the suburbs will look different from the path of an inner-city parish. Parishes that have a school or soup kitchen will need to consider how to engage the unique needs of those they already serve. You get the point.

The three elements that make a clear path effective and the Holy Spirit – the ultimate power source bringing it to life – will remain the same. Whatever the circumstances of your parish or ministry, your clear path will be a step-by-step framework that helps people move through the thresholds of conversion and discipleship. It will clearly highlight a few ministries so people can see their next steps. It will be connected so people have the accompaniment they need through the journey. Finally, and most importantly, it will be built and animated by the power of the Holy Spirit.

The Wild Goose

In the Celtic traditions of Scotland and Ireland, the Holy Spirit is sometimes referenced not as a gentle dove but as a wild goose. It is true that the Holy Spirit often comes upon us as a gentle dew or a dove, but the Celtic tradition highlights another aspect of the Spirit. He is wild. There is a passion, creativity, and unpredictability to the Holy Spirit's work, especially in evangelization.

This is where exercising discernment is crucial. Without discernment, determining next steps and identifying people and ministries can feel chaotic. (See Appendices III and IV for a simple prayer guide and discernment resources.)

Those who have embraced the journey to transform their parishes into missionary outposts consistently testify to the power of the Holy Spirit. He leads the way and calls us out of our comfort zones to new levels of faith and trust. It is exciting and surprising and among the deepest joys of those who set out to discern and build a clear path.

As you continue to read the description of a clear path in Part I and how to build it in Part II, I beg you to remember the Holy Spirit will lead the way. I would suggest as you read the case study in Part III you remember that the Holy Spirit is the main character. He is the mover and driver. He provides all we need just when we need it, but he often likes to be behind the scenes.

Returning to the two images of the Holy Spirit as the dove and the wild goose, I would like to affirm both aspects of the work of the Spirit. He is wild and creative and powerful and unpredictable. He is also gentle and unassuming. He draws our attention to the Father, the Son, and to the needs of our neighbors. I invite you to consider the journey you are embarking on as an extended adventure with the Spirit and embrace both facets of his action in your life. He will be your strength and your guide.

In the next few chapters, I will break down each of the key elements that make a clear path such an effective strategy for making and maturing disciples. These elements will provide a framework for building a clear path of discipleship designed specifically for your parish or ministry.

Questions for Reflection

1. How does a clear path foster collaboration?
2. How does a clear path help people take ownership of their spiritual journey?
3. How does a clear path help keep people from getting lost on the journey?
4. Which of the benefits do you find most attractive and motivating?
5. What other benefits do you envision if your parish developed a clear path?
6. What are the three elements of a clear path that make it so effective?
7. Do you tend to experience the Holy Spirit more often as gentle dove or wild goose?

Chapter 3
A Path Fostering Conversion

The first essential element of a clear path is that it fosters conversion by providing a framework with steps for growth through the thresholds. Following the wisdom of the Church on the process of evangelization, a clear path assists people as they move and grow in their spiritual journey.

Let us return to our simple definition. *A clear path of discipleship is a simple, step-by-step plan for making and maturing disciples by the power of the Holy Spirit.*

A clear path is a plan. It is a step-by-step plan because people typically grow one step at a time. Very few people arrive at Christian maturity without quite a few steps along the way. Just listen to someone tell the story of when they first decided to entrust themselves to Christ. They talk about the different people, conversations, and experiences that helped them on the journey. Each step led them closer to Jesus, and all the steps were connected. The key is providing a continuous pathway where the next steps are clear, and none are too far apart for an individual to traverse.

A clear path of discipleship considers the slow and often incremental progress individuals make in their faith journey. It works to intentionally provide the relationships, contexts, and ministries through which individuals can take their next step toward Christ. It is more than just an entry into the community or "getting involved." A clear path provides support for individuals to grow to *full maturity in Christ.*

The vision of Christian discipleship laid out by the New Testament exceeds the horizons we typically set to be a "good parishioner." The Lord has called everyone to the fullness of prayer and fruitfulness in their personal mission. Jesus never calls a disciple to follow him without also calling him or her to be fishers of men. As such, our plan to make disciples must include a plan to mature disciples into missionaries, who bear fruit in changed lives. The Lord does not just call us to be faithful – he calls us to be fruitful (Mt. 13:23, Jn. 15:16).

A clear path of discipleship considers the varied ways the Lord calls us and provides a process for growth into that fruitful maturity. It provides faithful disciples a context to be equipped for their personal ministry so that all may reach their full maturity in Christ. It also provides a ministry context for faithful disciples to accompany non-believers through the conversion process.

However, we must admit that even programs designated as "ministry" sometimes do not make or mature disciples. They keep people busy, but they do not draw them closer to full Christian maturity. A clear path of discipleship differs because it helps individuals through both the conversion process and through growth as they mature. It does not distract or overwhelm. It simply provides enough options so individuals can find and take their next steps.

The Four Steps of a Clear Path

One of the keys to developing a clear path is to think in terms of steps rather than programs. Programs are simply tools that create a context for ministry to happen. Steps refer to the types of ministries that foster growth in conversion and discipleship. Ideally, one ministry will be able to accommodate a substantial number of individuals through a particular step in the journey. Sometimes that ministry might need several options or programs to assist people in that threshold of the journey. Options are fine, but the options in that ministry must all work together to help individuals grow and move through that step in the path.

A clear path of discipleship, then, provides a sequential framework whereby the community intentionally helps individuals take their next steps closer to Christ. The steps on the path foster growth through the thresholds of conversion and discipleship.

A clear path of discipleship has four main steps: Relational Outreach, Conversion Moment, Faith Formation, and Evangelization Formation. The following image shows how these four steps correspond with the Thresholds of Conversion and Discipleship.

A Clear Path of Discipleship

Thresholds of Conversion and Discipleship

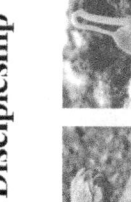

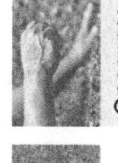

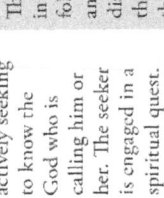

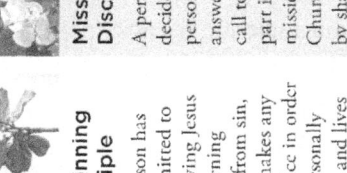

Trust
A person has a positive association with Jesus or an individual Catholic and may begin asking questions out of passive curiosity.

Openness
A person admits to a general need or desire for personal spiritual change. This is not the same as a commitment to specific changes.

Seeking
A person moves from being passive to actively seeking to know the God who is calling him or her. The seeker is engaged in a spiritual quest.

Decision
The decision, in faith, to follow Jesus as an obedient disciple in the midst of the Church, which brings about new life.

Beginning Disciple
A person has committed to following Jesus by turning away from sin, and makes any sacrifice in order to personally grow, and lives habits of the Christian life.

Missionary Disciple
A person has decided to personally answer the call to take part in the mission of the Church by sharing the Good News.

Fruitful Disciple
A person is fully equipped for lifelong Catholic mission and makes any sacrifice to help another person to grow spiritually.

| Relational Outreach | Conversion Moment | Faith Formation | Evangelization Formation |

Relational Outreach

Relational outreach is a ministry designed to build relationships of trust with individuals who are non-practicing, the fallen away, and even non-believers. It is designed to reach anyone who is not yet connected to the community of faith. It also provides a space for current disciples to introduce others to the community of faith in a non-threatening way. Relational outreach typically serves individuals at the thresholds of trust and openness. More than just hospitality for those who come to us, ministries at this step go out and provide invitations to those who are not a part of the community through authentic friendships. This often looks like fun and fellowship in homes and outside the parish.

In the case study in Part III of this book, you will see how a softball team provided a context for missionary disciples to *connect* with those who were not a part of their parish. Those relationships of trust became a bridge to the next step on the path. Relational outreach could be a regular play date for mothers with young children or a crafting club. It could be a series of neighborhood block parties or a food pantry delivered to those in need. What matters is space for conversation where mature missionary disciples can build bridges of trust with those who are not practicing their faith or are not believers. (To see an example of relational outreach, reference the case study in Part III beginning on page 168.)

Conversion Moment

A conversion moment is a ministry designed to foster an encounter with Jesus and a call to conversion. This may be a renewed encounter and deeper conversion, or it may be an initial conversion for those with no previous connection to the person of Jesus. Conversion moments typically serve individuals at the thresholds of seeking and decision. More than just a connection to the community, ministries in this step provide a clear proclamation of the Good News of God's love and mercy. This often happens in the context of a parish mission event or retreat. Conversion moments foster both initial conversion for non-believers and a renewed encounter for those who, though members of the community of faith, have never made an explicit adult decision to follow Christ.

In the case study, you will see how a weekend retreat, called "Awakening," consistently provides a powerful moment of encounter for participants to *know* the Lord personally. (To see an example of a conversion moment, reference the case study in Part III beginning on page 174.)

Faith Formation

Faith formation includes ministries designed to support disciples as they grow in the knowledge and habits of the Christian life. Faith formation typically serves individuals at the thresholds of decision and beginning disciple. Ministries in this step provide more than information. They give context for transformation. They offer catechesis, formation in prayer, and accompaniment in how to live as a disciple. Faith formation often happens in the context of small group gatherings and dynamic formation classes.

In the case study, you will see how small group gatherings called, "Grow Groups," provide a context for a new disciple to *grow* and mature in prayer and understanding of the faith. The genuine friendship of mature disciples provides models for how to live as a disciple of Jesus. (To see an example of faith formation, reference the case study in Part III beginning on page 181.)

Evangelization Formation

Evangelization formation is any ministry designed to equip disciples as they are sent out on mission through the power of the Holy Spirit. Evangelization formation typically serves individuals at the thresholds of missionary disciple and fruitful disciple. More than just evangelization theory, ministries at this step provide practical training in evangelization skills and the works of mercy. They also provide individuals with a personalized awareness of their gifting from the Holy Spirit for mission. Evangelization formation often happens in the context of mentorship and group training events.

In the case study, you will see how group trainings called "Upper Rooms," along with a retreat focused on the Holy Spirit, a ministry gift assessment, and simple mentorship combine to equip disciples to *go* out on mission. (To see an example of evangelization formation, reference the case study in Part III beginning on page 190.)

Adapting the Steps to Your Parish

DISCLAIMER: A clear path of discipleship will vary from parish to parish. There will be different ministries and programs that make up each step on the path. The number of steps may also vary. There is nothing magical about these four steps. They simply represent the most common types of ministries needed to help individuals move through the thresholds of conversion and discipleship.

A parish's clear path will also be unique as it reflects its specific parish culture. There may be a particular emphasis on healing, or intellectual formation, or the corporal works of mercy. A clear path can and should reflect the needs of a particular parish's mission field and the unique gifting of that faith community. *What really matters is that the ministries comprising your clear path help individuals in your community grow through the thresholds.*

For the sake of consistency, I will use these four steps to illustrate a clear path. The concepts are essential, but please remember that the names and the number of these steps could vary according to the needs of your parish.

In Part II you will learn how to create a simple visual representation of your clear path. You will also receive suggestions for creating a simple verbal mantra to communicate the steps in your clear path. In the case study in Part III, you will see how St. Mary's Parish used their mantra, **"Connect, Know, Grow, and Go,"** to communicate the ministry steps of their clear path. The following image ties the specific ministries of St. Mary's clear path to this mantra.

A Path for Movement

Part of the power of a clear path of discipleship is that it fosters movement and growth in a person's spiritual journey.

The Lord loves us right where we are, but he loves us too much to leave us there. His vision for our lives is often much greater than our own. We are the ones with small expectations. And we often get stuck. A clear path creates a culture and a structure to help people move and grow.

Consider the difference between a shopping mall and a school. In some respects, the architecture is not that different. There are long hallways, common areas for meals, and compartmentalized rooms with various offerings in each. The difference is when visiting a mall there are no expectations that visiting one store will require you to visit all the others. Unless you are a compulsive shopper, you will visit a handful of stores and then leave. A school, on the other hand, is designed to help students move, grow, and mature. It is a disappointment if someone visits second grade but never moves on to third grade. There is an expectation for movement and growth. A clear path can help create the culture and structure to facilitate movement and growth in our parishes.

Think about hiking in the mountains. Some of the most beautiful lakes and meadows are hidden, out of sight from the base of the mountain. Left to wander through the trees on their own, most people would never reach these beautiful places. Fortunately, people are not on their own. Maps, trail guides, fellow hikers, and a clear trail all provide help along the way. A lot of work goes into helping ensure this hidden beauty is not missed.

What if you were to translate this to the process of making disciples in our parishes? What might be the difference in growth, maturity and changed lives for those hungering for growth? What might be the difference for those who seem uninterested or disengaged? There is a temptation to assume that lack of growth is a fundamental lack of desire. That may or may not be true. Making things a little easier for people to grow and mature makes a significant difference. A clear path removes obstacles and makes the next steps for growth easier to find and take.

One Step at a Time

When a parish or specific ministry has fully developed and connected these four steps, a person at any threshold of the spiritual journey can easily take their next step. The ministries that make up a parish's clear path provide the context to grow in their journey through the thresholds of conversion and discipleship.

Parishes that have fully developed their clear path of discipleship typically have one, or possibly two, ministries for each step. These ministries collaborate to make disciples in that parish. All other ministries, programming, and activities somehow support making disciples on this clear path. Some provide indirect support like facilities. Some, such as youth ministry and religious education, mirror the clear path for specific demographics. Others provide additional on-ramps to the clear path. Taken together, the clear path and the other ministries of the parish work together to provide a clear next step for a person at any threshold of the spiritual journey.

For some of you, the task of building a clear path may already seem overwhelming. It might feel like there is already too much to do and not enough time. Stay with me. I will address how to build a clear path in Part II.

The key will be to gather a group of leaders to help as you patiently build your path one step at a time. You are not going to do this alone, and you probably are not starting from scratch. Much good work is already being done in parishes. A clear path will help a parish structure itself so the fruitful evangelization already happening can increase and bear even more fruit in fully mature missionary disciples.

Dispelling Misconceptions

At this point, it might be helpful to talk about what a clear path of discipleship is *not*. Trying new things can be hard and a little intimidating. Often, it is simply new to our current experience of parish life. There is potential for misconceptions to confuse our understanding of the essential elements of a clear path.

Not a Fad

A clear path is not a man-made fad. It is just another expression of the timeless wisdom of the Church for making disciples. Although the terminology around a clear path of discipleship is new, the principles and practices involved are as old as the Church itself. In fact, a clear path of discipleship is an intentional rediscovery of the timeless practice of the Church to make disciples. If you are familiar with the process of Christian initiation through which adults enter the Catholic Church, you will notice the similarities. A clear path aligns with what the Church has always taught about how people become Christians.

In Church language, it is called the catechumenal model, and it follows the process of evangelization laid out in the National Directory for Catechesis by the bishops of the United States. You will also find the principles and practices behind a clear path of discipleship in the process developed by the early Church to bring someone into the Catholic faith. The Church's re-discovery and re-articulation of this ancient practice after the Second Vatican Council is finding yet another expression in the concept of a clear path of discipleship.

Those familiar with new ecclesial movements, which have been springing up in the Church, will notice a similar pattern. Ecclesial movements, whether they be dedicated to the evangelization of young people or some other group, often have a clear path of discipleship built into the movement. By this I mean all the members of the movement know very clearly how new members connect relationally to the community. They know where the gospel is preached and where people tend to experience conversion. They have regular, clear, and intentional time set aside for forming disciples, and they have regular, clear contexts set aside for equipping disciples for mission.

Parishes can learn from this timeless wisdom. In many ways, a clear path is simply the old made new again.

Not a Shortcut

A clear path of discipleship is not a promise that the life of discipleship will be easy or quick. Maybe you are thinking, "My journey of discipleship was long and confusing with lots of twists and turns. It was anything but easy, and it certainly didn't appear clear." Exactly. The Christian life is not easy. Following the Lord's lead can be difficult. The goal of a clear path of discipleship is to simplify the path so the process is no harder than it needs to be.

A clear path of discipleship cannot magically make and mature disciples by eliminating the journey people must take through the thresholds. What it can do is provide clear next steps for those who are ready to move and grow. A clear path can help remove some of the confusion people face as they seek to follow the Lord on their journey of faith. It can provide crucial support at key moments along the journey in the form of ministries and accompaniment. It can help keep people from getting lost or stuck on the way. A clear path can significantly accelerate growth in the process of conversion and discipleship, but it is not a shortcut.

Some parish leaders hear the call to develop a clear path of discipleship and feel overwhelmed at the scope of change. They may fear that everything needs to change overnight. Other leaders *want* the change to happen overnight and discount the time it will take to develop a clear path of discipleship. Neither are effective leadership. It is normal for the full process of building a clear path to take three to five years of ongoing discernment and implementation.

Before you build a highway, it is okay to start with a dirt path. The Holy Spirit is already at work in the hearts and minds of people in our neighborhoods and parishes. In many ways, building a clear path will require discernment of where the Lord is already at work and a commitment to intentionally cooperate with that work even if it is just a dirt path. It will require patience and steadfast commitment. The Lord can do amazing things when we patiently persevere in following his lead for making disciples, but the day-to-day labor of building a clear path does not feel quick.

Bringing Our Mission Statements to Life

A clear path of discipleship is where mission, evangelization, and discipleship all come together. It has been more than 30 years since Pope Saint John Paul II called for a new evangelization. Undoubtedly, his prophetic call is emerging in the many new ecclesial movements. We must, however, admit that "a new springtime of evangelization" is not most people's experience in the typical parish yet. Even the best mission statements do not automatically make disciples.

Back in 2011, the Synod of Bishops drew attention to this phenomenon. "Despite the fact that the expression [the New Evangelization] is widely known in the Church, it has failed to be accepted fully and totally," they wrote.[17] The "failure" of the new evangelization to be implemented is, in part, due to the gap between our mission statements and the behaviors that drive our experience. A clear path of discipleship has the potential to change that experience so that our mission statements come to life in our ministries and bear fruit in changed lives.

A clear path of discipleship is a pathway for making disciples, but as the name would suggest, it must be clear. In the next chapter, we will zero in on the importance of the element of clarity.

---

[17] *The New Evangelization for the Transmission of the Christian Faith*, Lineamenta for the Synod of Bishops' XIII Ordinary General Assembly, February 2011, #5. © Dicastero per la Comunicazione-Libreria Editrice Vaticana.

Questions for Reflection

1. What are the ministry steps that typically make up a clear path? What is each step designed to do?

2. How does a clear path foster movement and growth in people's faith journey?

3. How might having a clear path of discipleship in your parish differ from your experience of parish life up to this point?

4. A clear path is not a fad. Where else can you find the principles behind a clear path expressed in the teachings of the Church?

5. A clear path is not a shortcut. How does a clear path make the spiritual journey easier?

6. What is your parish's mission statement? How does that manifest in practice?

Chapter 4
A Path Providing Clarity

The second key element of a clear path of discipleship is clarity. A clear path provides clarity by highlighting a few ministries for simplicity and maximum fruitfulness.

There is power in clarity, especially in our overly busy and noisy world. A clear path provides clarity for both insiders and outsiders. That clarity flows, in part, from the limited number of ministries that make up the clear path itself. It also flows from the intentional focus by those ministries on supporting individuals at specific thresholds of their faith journey. Finally, the clarity flows from consistency in communication about the clear path.

Busy, Busy, Busy

In the 1980s, cultural commentators began to notice that one of the greatest threats to family life in America was the increasingly frenzied pace of life. That was probably true in the '80s, and yet, the pace of life has done nothing but accelerate since then.

It may seem hard to believe, but no one had a smartphone in the '80s. Steve Jobs released the first iPhone in 2007. No one had social media. Facebook began in 2004.

Everyone is working longer and harder than ever before. Ask almost anyone how they are doing, and you will get the same response: "Busy." No one seems to be immune. From children to grandparents, our time and attention spans are less than they have ever been...because we are busy.

This has major consequences for how we minister to our stressed and busy friends and neighbors. We have met the enemy, and he is us. Our own lives are so busy and noisy that we do not have time to really listen to the Lord or to our neighbors. Our friends and neighbors do not have time to connect with us so the witness of our lives can arouse some curiosity for the gospel. This is a real problem since the best way to do outreach and to evangelize is through authentic friendships.

Before this section devolves into a rant about the pace of life, let me come back to the clear path and clarity. A clear path is an intentionally countercultural move to simplify programming and clarify messaging. It is an attempt to cut through the noise and clutter of our modern culture so people can connect with the Lord and each other.

This stands in marked contrast to the typical programming approach of providing countless opportunities for people to "get involved." It also stands in marked contrast to the typical communication approach that gives equal airtime for all parish activities.

Many of the ministries that make up the clear path have been around for decades. What is perhaps new is the importance of clarity. Clarity was never unimportant, but now it is essential. Clarity that flows from simplicity, focus, and consistency is more important than ever. If you really lean into making a *clear* path, it will be countercultural. I promise it will be worth the effort, and the first to benefit from that clarity will be insiders.

Clarity for Insiders

Fundamentally, insiders will need clarity about *why* there is a need for a clear path of discipleship. The why of building a clear path of discipleship will highlight making disciples as the essential mission of the Church. That why must also make this mission personal for current members. It is our mission, and it is for our friends, our family, and our neighbors. It is about changing the lives of people we love with the Good News of Jesus Christ.

At a practical level, insiders will also need to know what specific ministries make up the steps on your path. They need this information if they are going to effectively serve as ambassadors of the community and attend to the needs of the individuals in front of them. Without much effort, current members will know how to help others take their next step in your community.

Almost anyone in a parish community can be used at a key moment to help someone else recognize their next step in the journey. That is the ideal. This is only possible, however, in a context of clarity and simplicity. To help others find and move to their next step, insiders must have clarity about what is offered and a simple way to share it with others.

In Part II, I will cover how a parish can develop a simple verbal mantra and a simple visual image to help provide clarity for insiders so they can help others find their next steps.

Clarity in Simplicity

A clear path of discipleship is limited in the number of ministries and programs by design. Its simplicity is at the service of clarity. In a day and age when we are overwhelmed with choices, simplicity is powerful. Most parishes lack the resources of people, finances, and facilities to run an infinite number of ministries and programs. Given the cultural tendency of Americans to try to do more, clarity in the form of simplicity must be chosen and protected.

This is not to say that all the activity of the parish must somehow fit into a clear path of discipleship. All the activities that happen in our parishes do not directly serve people's growth as disciples. That is okay. Mowing the lawn and waxing the floors are good and necessary work even if they do not directly contribute to making disciples. There may be many activities, and even "ministries," which continue at a parish but are not a part of the clear path of discipleship. You do not need to cut everything else, but you do need to vigorously work to keep your clear path simple and uncluttered.

Simplicity in the steps of your clear path is key to effectiveness. The research of Travis Bradshaw found a striking correlation between simplicity and growth in churches. Churches with fewer ministries and programs actually can grow more than those with more offerings.[18] Bradshaw initially hypothesized churches with more ministries, events, and programming would have higher growth. The research showed the opposite to be true. Bradshaw found that the highest percentage of growth came from churches with fewer programs and offerings. Did you catch that? The simpler a church is the more it can grow. Although that finding might initially be surprising, a little reflection confirms why this is the case.

A multiplicity of programs spreads resources and leaders thin. Less programming concentrates the best of our time and energy, as well as our financial and leadership resources, into the ministries that really help people grow. As it turns out, less really is more in the church world.

Our own experience confirms this phenomenon. Back when shopping centers were still crowded, there were stores that sold fragrant candles and perfumed lotion. You probably have some stuck in the back of a closet or cabinet somewhere in your home. Those stores had an overwhelming number of fragrance choices. The stores themselves began to realize the multiplicity of choices they offered was their own worst enemy.

At first, the stores would offer a sample spread of their products right out front as shoppers would pass. Sometimes there would be almost a dozen choices. Over time, experience demonstrated the decision to buy decreased based on the increasing number of choices. After the third sniff, people would get overwhelmed and just walk away. The stores found they sold more products if they offered only a small handful of choices out front. As it turns out, less really is more outside the church world too.

The temptation to offer too many choices is especially strong in the church world. We mistakenly offer an

---

[18] Travis H. Bradshaw, *Evangelistic Churches: Geographic, Demographic, and Marketing Variables That Facilitate Their Growth*, Ph.D., diss., University of Florida, 2000.

overabundance of choices thinking "something for everyone" will improve engagement. You can see examples of this everywhere. Just look at your church's public bulletin board or website's "Get Involved" tab. You will see an overwhelming number of choices.

People can attend the "Lifetime Retreat," the knitting club, men's golf, volunteer for the fish fry, and a dozen types of formation. People can join a video series on the book of James or be a youth chaperone. They are invited to serve the poor, coordinate the endowment dinner, be in the prayer class, and on and on and on.

How would a newcomer know where to begin? How would someone who has been a part of the community for years know what is next for their own spiritual growth? People are just too busy. The world is noisy. We must be different. We must be simple and clear.

Please do not misunderstand this call for simplicity. Almost every parish ministry can find a place in the mission of the parish, *but not every parish ministry can be part of a clear path of discipleship.* If all the ministries available were included, the path would not be clear.

At some point the time will come to identify ministries and activities that are not part of the clear path. As part of the building process, some ministries and activities might need to be paused or pruned. This comes later. I will address pruning in Part II in the chapter on alignment. For now, I hope you are growing in the conviction that your clear path must be simple.

Both insiders and outsiders should be able to quickly assess how newcomers get connected. It should be crystal clear how this faith community fosters conversion. Key moments designed to foster growth in the knowledge and habits of discipleship should be clearly designated. Finally, forming and equipping missionary disciples as leaders should be clearly designated as well.

Clarity is one of the key elements that makes a clear path of discipleship so effective in making and maturing disciples. In my estimation, this is the hardest for pastors and parish leaders to embrace because clarity requires saying "no." That might disappoint some people. Clarity requires an intentional choice to offer less so the path to growth and maturity is clear. There is no doubt clarity is countercultural, but it is not unorthodox. Jesus was a master of clarity and simplicity. It is okay to imitate him. As you seek to imitate Jesus' simplicity and clarity, be sure to remember his compassion as well. It is important to remain firm in our pursuit of simplicity, but we must communicate the changes we make with sensitivity. In Part II, we will spend considerable time on how to communicate well when building your clear path.

As we close this section, I encourage you to remember the individuals who try to navigate our sometimes complex and confusing array of programs.

The journey of faith can be hard. Life is better with Christ, but even after we have made an intentional decision, most of us would not describe the rest of the journey as easy. That is all the more reason to make sure we do not unnecessarily confuse and clutter the choices available to individuals within our community of faith. Do not be afraid to choose clarity through simplicity.

Clarity in Focus

Programs that make up a clear path of discipleship must also be clear about who they are focused on serving. *Programs need to be clearly designed for individuals at specific thresholds in the process of conversion and discipleship.* Events and programs that are designed for everyone rarely contribute to the growth of individuals. When we create specific contexts for individuals at specific points on the journey, growth tends to happen with more consistency. Our labor is not the ultimate source of growth in the Christian life; that is the work of the Holy Spirit. Rather, our role is to intentionally be present in moments where the Spirit can do what we already know he desires to do.

This is not so different than the classic spiritual advice to pray with specificity. The Lord already knows what we need before we ask. He knows our desires better than we do, but often in his mysterious providence, he withholds what we need until we ask. Indeed, he often withholds what we need until we ask with passion and precision. He is a good father. He does this to make it even clearer to us that he is indeed the source of every good and perfect gift. The specificity of our prayer serves only to remind us that he does indeed desire to provide for us in a personal and particular way. The same is true of our efforts to care for individuals within our faith community. The more we create moments specific to what those individuals need, the more visibly we can see God move.

It must be acknowledged that this clarity of purpose for most parish ministries is not common. Although almost every ministry and program would benefit from some intentional reflection on who they aim to serve, that is not strictly necessary for every ministry. It is, however, essential for those ministries that will make up a clear path of discipleship. Leaders must clearly know what threshold of the spiritual journey their ministry serves. So too, parishioners must know which thresholds the ministries on the clear path aim to serve. In fact, the goal is that even non-members can recognize who ministries are designed to serve.

Clarity for Outsiders

Once we have become clear in our own minds about the purpose of ministries and programs, we can begin to communicate that clarity to outsiders. This is where a clear path of discipleship goes public. Visual icons, mantras like "Encounter–Know–Proclaim," and other communication tools play a key role.

It is this clarity about the steps on the clear path that helps newcomers self-assess their next step. It can be hard for most parish leaders to recognize and connect with newcomers because visitors often come and leave quickly. This is especially hard in larger faith communities. What if your community's communication was so clear that outsiders knew where to get started? It is one thing to have something for individuals at every part of the journey. It is quite another thing for outsiders to find those options and to connect.

Clarity in Consistent Communication

Let us consider the metaphor of a parish's programming as a network of roads with a main highway, signage, frontage roads, and side streets. In a well-designed system, all the parts work together to help people move from one place to another without getting lost along the way. A clear path is like the main highway. Main highways are often *elevated* roadways. They are often built just a bit higher than surrounding roadways and terrain. In like manner, if a parish's clear path is going to remain clear, it must be elevated. The ministries of a clear path must be more prominent. To keep the clear path more prominent, you will need to be vigilant, consistent, and simple in your communication.

Consistency in communication is one of the most essential elements for creating clarity for a clear path of discipleship. The words, phrases, and visual images that communicate a clear path must be consistent. In like manner, the mission of the parish to make disciples must be communicated with consistency. That mission is the reason the clear path exists. Young people especially are attracted to a compelling *why*. For example, a parish could provide clarity with a simple phrase, such as: "Helping everyone take their next step in their relationship with Christ." That phrase should show up everywhere. You should see it printed on everything, and you might hear it several times on a Sunday.

There are many reasons why consistency in communication is so important. We live in a very noisy and distracted world. People need to hear something multiple times before the message begins to register. Secondly, a clear path of discipleship is still a very new concept in most parishes.

Consistency in communication will help both insiders and outsiders understand the purpose of a clear path.

Finally, consistency in communication is important because, God willing, there will always be someone new starting the journey. As new people arrive at your parish, they need to hear the same messages if they are to begin to find their place and feel at home. Without consistent communication, they will never "catch up" with the community.

In many ways, providing clear communication about your clear path is a form of hospitality. When you land at an airport, hospitality is often provided in the form of simple and consistent communication. Signs in the airport help direct you where to go. Airline staff provide directions about what is happening and where you need to be. Veteran travelers and others familiar with flying tend to form a herd that new travelers can follow. Taken together, good signs, clear instructions, and a reliable guide can provide a hospitable orientation to a new airport.

Now, I know not all airports feel hospitable. The communication is not always clear. That is the point. We notice the difference when communication is clear, especially when we land somewhere the first time. If we are going to make disciples, new people are going to land in our churches. Does our communication provide the clarity they need to begin to feel at home and find their way?

In Part II, I will spend a whole chapter on how to communicate your clear path of discipleship in a clear and compelling way.

Dispelling Misconceptions

As we close this chapter, there are a few misconceptions specific to the element of clarity in a clear path that should be addressed.

Not a Multiplicity of Programs

A clear path is not simply a multiplicity of programs. Too many programs are not helpful, and it is not a clear path of discipleship. A clear path of discipleship is strategic, not haphazard. It is a *clear* and connected pathway where an individual can move and grow through the process of conversion and discipleship. That clarity does not require a multiplicity of programs. In fact, a multiplicity of programs is usually unhelpful.

If we are honest with ourselves, most of us would admit we are a little tired. If you are in parish leadership and reading this book, you are likely already running near 100% of capacity or over. Adding more programs to help people get connected might initially seem helpful in providing "on-ramps" for those at various thresholds of their faith journey, but most of us lack the energy and capable leaders to do so. Besides, on-ramps do no good if they do not connect and lead somewhere.

The limitation of our capacity is actually a blessing because a clear path is not about offering programs to suit every taste and preference. Remember the research? Too many programs and ministries dissipate our energy and complicate the path, making it unclear. Offering fewer choices with excellence enables us to have a greater impact.

Not Cutting All Other Ministry

A common misconception about the element of clarity is that implementing a clear path means cutting all your existing ministries to start over. That is not the case. Building a clear path of discipleship is a commitment to good leadership and to shepherding souls so the ministries of your parish work together to make disciples. Some ministries may need to be paused or pruned so others can grow and flourish, but this requires careful discernment. Often, a step on the clear path can be built out of an existing ministry. That step gets emphasized and highlighted in a new way as an excellent place where people can grow.

Some ministries will help make disciples in a more central way than others. The ministries that form your clear path of discipleship must take a more prominent role in the life of the parish, but almost every type of ministry can find a place. It can be a good thing to have different ministries in a parish if they ultimately serve the mission: making disciples.

Again, you could imagine the ministries of the parish serving like a road network. The ministries that make up a clear path of discipleship might be the main highway. Other ministries and contexts are like the side streets and frontage roads. Those frontage roads and side streets serve their purpose when they connect people to the main highway. In fact, they are especially valuable as on-ramps for those who are at different points in the journey. The only thing you want to avoid is roads that lead to nowhere. As part of the process of building a clear path, you will eventually work toward alignment, so every ministry contributes to the overall mission to make and mature disciples.

The Stakes

The stakes for our efforts to build a clear path could not be higher. The need to build a clear path of discipleship is about more than keeping our parish institutions going. It is about eternity and the reality of heaven and hell.

The truth is heaven and hell are both real. Jesus talked about hell. He talked about hell a lot. He talked about it more than heaven, and his descriptions are more vivid. He is not trying to convince us that the descriptions he uses are the reality in hell (e.g., worms that never die). He wants to impress upon us the uncomfortable fact that *hell is for real*. Our lives require a decision, and that decision has consequences for eternity. It has consequences not just for us but for countless others.

In personal evangelization, we can be tempted to let the fear of being awkward keep us from sharing our faith. I get it. I feel that too. Sometimes, it stops me. Sometimes, I live bravely and am reminded that it was more awkward in my head than in reality. When the fear of awkwardness creeps in, I love to remind people that eternity is worth the awkwardness.

There is an analogous fear in parish evangelization. We fear clarity. We fear clarity because it forces us to say 'no' to something. If we are honest, it may force us to say 'no' to quite a few things, even good things that are not most needed at that time. It can be hard or seem like we are playing favorites. Somebody might get confused or angry.

Since we are talking about clarity, let us be clear: *we cannot let the fear of saying 'no' stand in the way of effectively making disciples*. Nothing should stand in the way of clarity about how people encounter Jesus and grow as disciples in your community. The mission to make disciples is too important. Eternity hangs in the balance.

In the next chapter, I will begin to explore how a clear path is connected. I will discuss how to find and form leaders who can serve as "connectors." They help facilitate the very personal and individual journey people take through the clear path.

Questions for Reflection

1. What does the research say about the correlation between the number of ministries a church offers and its growth?
2. What are the problems with offering a multiplicity of choices in parish programming?
3. How clear is the focus of specific ministries, events, and programs in your parish?
4. How well do current parishioners know where to connect people for their next step in your parish?
5. How do you think newcomers experience the options available at your parish?
6. What might be at stake if a parish or ministry cannot be clear in how it helps people grow and mature as a part of their community?

Chapter 5
A Path Offering Connection

The third key element of an effective clear path of discipleship is that the path is *connected*. A clear path offers connection between highlighted ministries so no one gets lost on the journey. That connection happens in two ways. First, the ministries themselves are designed to connect to one another so they can assist individuals to move from one step on the path to another. Secondly, connection is brought to life by individuals who serve as "connectors" inviting and accompanying individuals on their journey. We will take some time to break down both ways a clear path is connected.

Connected Ministries

The ministries forming the steps of a clear path of discipleship must connect to one another. They must be designed as sequential pieces of the whole pathway to make and mature disciples. The people associated with the ministries not only understand the role *their* ministry plays, but they understand the role *other* ministries play in helping people move and grow.

A clear path helps a pastor and parish leaders shepherd people through the steps of their personal growth. In a way, the connected structure of the ministry steps extends the shepherding role of pastors. Like Jesus, the Good Shepherd, we must be willing to go and chase the lost, but wouldn't it be better if we could keep them from getting lost in the first place?

I am reminded of the importance of the handoff for a relay team at a track and field event. If you have ever watched the relays, they are among the most exciting and often unpredictable races. Speed alone does not determine the winner. The key moment comes during the handoff when one runner passes the baton to another. A bad handoff or a dropped baton can mean the loss of the race no matter how fast the individual runners may be. Real success depends on the handoff.

The same is true for the ministries that make up the steps of a clear path. Their ultimate success lies not simply in faithfully fostering the growth of individuals at that threshold of the journey but in helping those individuals connect as they move to their next step. As such, ministries must intentionally practice the handoff as if they were part of a relay team.

The handoff is not just passing a person or information along. It is the connection. Commitment to making the connection by both ministries involved is vital. Follow-up that feels like invitation, inclusion, and genuine care helps to move people from one threshold to another. A successful handoff may require hard questions, such as, "Can it be done with the current staff or volunteers?" Again, discernment is required.

The leaders who coordinate ministries at each step must have a plan for helping those who are ready to move to their next step. The leaders must know each other and trust each other. They must work proactively to ensure a smooth transition. Some of that connection can be provided by sharing names and contact information as participants move from one ministry to another. That is a start. More important than simply sharing contact information, leaders will facilitate connections through relationships.

Practically, this may look like a missionary disciple joining a beginning disciple as they move onto their next ministry step. It could look like an informational visit and invitation from the next step ministry. It should feel like a personal introduction of one friend to another. Regardless of how the connection is made, it must provide a clear invitation from the next step ministry and a clear explanation of the benefits that ministry offers for those ready to move.

To foster a smooth handoff, ministry leaders must realize that the real test of their success is how effectively they can facilitate growth and movement. Success is no longer about simply collecting more participants for a particular ministry.

Real success is about an individual's growth, movement, and connection to their next step on the path.

To provide that type of a connected path, individuals who serve as connectors are essential. Connectors function as living bridges who invite people from one step to another. Let us look at how to find and form connectors.

Finding Connectors

Leaders who serve as connectors bring your clear path of discipleship to life. They help shepherd other individuals from one threshold of the journey to another. In the words of Pope Francis, they provide accompaniment, so people do not get lost or stuck on the way. They are parishioners who have both clarity about what is offered at the parish and the skills necessary to accompany others through the key moments of transition from one threshold to another.

Connectors come in many different shapes and sizes. Their only ministry may be as connectors, or they may provide leadership within a ministry. They may be extremely social or a great listener. Some will serve in a formal capacity. Others will simply connect people as part of their personality. It does not matter if they are introverted or extroverted, connectors are key to bringing a clear path of discipleship to life. *Whatever their personality, connectors will embody the personal love of God to individuals as they grow and mature in your community of faith.*

Most of our faith communities struggle to find leaders capable of accompanying individuals on their personal journey of faith. Often, these leaders are spread among a multiplicity of ministries that may or may not actually make disciples. The ability to gather and concentrate key leaders for mission is essential for a parish to become a missional community. Trying to maintain a multiplicity of poorly defined programs puts a strain on your most precious and scarce resource: *missionary disciples*.

The more programs and ministries offered, the harder it is for connectors to help people bridge the gap to their next step. Connectors must be able to recognize when individuals are ready to move forward in order to invite and assist that movement to the next step. With too many choices, it would be like trying to help new students on their first day of school find a locker if the lockers were spread randomly throughout the school building. To further complicate matters, the students enter the building from every direction – side, back, and front doors. They also arrive at various times of day. In this example, no matter how hard the connectors work to help, many new students would get lost.

If a parish is going to help people move and grow through the various thresholds of discipleship, there also must be connectors who are able to provide invitation and accompaniment throughout that journey, particularly at the key moments when individuals are transitioning from one step to another. All of this cannot fall on the pastor or even the pastor and a few specially selected staff members. Thankfully, the Lord provides those who can assist in this shepherding role.

Some individuals have a natural gift for connecting with others. Some individuals even have a *supernatural* gift for connecting with others. They consistently help others move and grow. They may or may not be extroverts, but they will always have a heart for people. Individuals with the gifting to serve as connectors are often already serving this function in an informal way. Individuals who serve as connectors will often be good listeners. They will have an instinctive reverence for the unique timing of another individual's journey of faith, and they will know how to make sincere invitations.

Ultimately, the best way to find connectors is with prayer. The Lord specifically asks us to pray to the Father to send out laborers. Prayer does at least two things in helping us find leaders who can serve as connectors. First, we believe the Lord moves in the hearts and minds of individuals when we pray. He endows individuals with the gifts necessary for the calling he is giving. He does something new. Secondly, we get eyes to see what the Lord has already provided before we thought to ask.

Leaders are often already at work connecting. We need to look for individuals serving as leaders, even if their service is outside the parish community. Watch for individuals who are already connecting, even if the connections seem simply social and not explicitly at the service of someone's growth in faith.

Inviting Connectors

The key to empowering connectors is to explicitly invite them to serve as connectors. Ironically, even those who are already informally connecting with people may not recognize this habit in themselves. You should expect the need to bolster their confidence. Although some of that confidence will come naturally during your efforts to equip leaders as connectors, some must come at the very beginning with a clear and personal invitation to serve as a connector. A good invitation to serve will have several key characteristics:

Personal – Any invitation to serve, in this case as a connector, must be personal. Take time to reflect on the connector characteristic you specifically see in this person. Keep in mind, introverts may initially find it hard to imagine themselves serving as connectors. It might simply be that they are a good listener or that they have a common background with a key group of individuals who are often disconnected. *"I think you could really make a great connector for some of the young dads in the parish. You are standing at the back of church holding a fussy baby anyway. Why not try to make a connection as you stand there?"*

The Need – People must be reminded of the need. It is not that people are unaware of the need, but sometimes we can fail to recognize that things do not have to be this way. The fact young dads are often disconnected from their faith does not have to be an immoveable fact of life. Standing at the back of church with those young dads might just be an opportunity for someone to have influence in someone else's life... if we have eyes to see it. Your invitation should help people see the deeper need. *"You know more than most that it can get lonely once you start having children. The demands of work and caring for a growing family can overwhelm us and keep us from going deeper in our faith. It does not have to be that way."*

The Call – Every invitation to serve within the Church should at some level be an invitation to hear a call from the Lord. As such, we want to invite Jesus into the conversation and encourage others to invite him into their own discernment. We do not want to persuade people to serve because we asked them. We only seek to be a conduit for the Lord's calling to serve. *"I have been asking the Lord who might be a good connector for our young dads, and you came to mind. Would you be willing to pray about this for a couple of days? After that we can talk through if you think this is what the Lord is asking."*

Equipping Leaders as Connectors

So, how can you develop individuals who can assist the pastor in this type of shepherding of souls? An evangelization formation ministry will help you develop those who are gifted as connectors. That formation will have at least three elements. First, connectors must develop a general awareness of the thresholds of conversion and discipleship. Second, they must know and understand the parish ministries offered for each step of the clear path so they can make meaningful invitations. Third, they must model the maturity of fruitful disciples, serving both as living signposts and as trail guides for the journey.

The first two elements of formation go hand in hand. Awareness of the ministries offered by your parish's clear path will rest on the foundational understanding of the thresholds. In some ways, the thresholds are the why of a clear path of discipleship. The thresholds are a framework for understanding the process individual people go through in their journey of faith. As a result, they provide the rationale for why one ministry leads to another. To introduce individuals to the ministry steps offered by your parish's clear path of discipleship, you must first provide orientation to the thresholds of conversion and discipleship.

That orientation can take a variety of forms, but it is best if it takes place in a simple and straightforward manner. Ideally, individuals can begin to discover the thresholds in an interactive way.

For more information on how to introduce the framework of the thresholds, go to the Resources tab at clearpathbook.com. There you will find a fun and interactive game that teaches the thresholds.

Additionally, your orientation to the specific ministries that make up the steps of a clear path in your parish must be personal. That is, the individual leaders who facilitate the various programs within the parish must get to know one another. The ministries and programs of a clear path of discipleship cannot be siloed. They are highly interdependent, and as such, the leaders must have a good working relationship and connection to one another. The best way to facilitate this connection relies on the timeless wisdom of our faith communities – starting with food.

Gather the key leaders from each ministry for a meal and give them an opportunity to share the story of what the Lord is doing in and through their labors. It is crucial that this event highlights the interdependence of each specific ministry. A gathering of these ministry leaders is not the time for competition about who has the best story or the most participants. It is about fostering understanding and appreciation so everyone can serve as an effective connector. When leaders know, understand, and appreciate one another, those connections happen much more easily.

Character of Connectors

Leaders will serve most fruitfully as connectors if they are already living as faithful disciples. At a minimum, they must have made a firm decision for the person of Jesus Christ, but do not expect them to be sinless. They should be growing in prayer and the habits of discipleship. At the most basic level, they should be faithful to the teachings of the Church and live a life filled with prayer and the sacraments.

That faithfulness in their life will likely have been fostered by the gift of another mature disciple, who served as a mentor through key periods of their own faith journey. That mentorship may or may not have been explicit. It may have just been the informal witness of a grandparent, coach, or coworker. It might also have been through participation in some formal program designed to mature disciples. The formality of accompaniment that a connector experienced really does not matter. What matters is their faithfulness to the Church, their docility to the Holy Spirit, and their commitment to walking with others. Connectors will intuitively know how to accompany people to deeper faithfulness because they have experienced that accompaniment themselves. *In other words, they will return the love they have received in their own journey of faith.*

I highly recommend looking for individuals who have experience in formation with one of the movements in the Church mentioned earlier. There are also countless other Spanish speaking movements. They are often untapped treasures. Regardless of their specific background, connectors have likely experienced formation and accompaniment themselves.

It is important to remember that typical parish life can be challenging for individuals who have experienced vibrant faith as part of an ecclesial movement. They love the Church, and they come to the parish for sacraments. They come in the hopes of finding fellowship, but sometimes they remain outside of parish life.

Sometimes, they find it difficult to engage in the mainstream life of the parish because it is so different from the experiences that formed them as disciples. Look carefully for individuals who display deep faith but who are not yet serving in leadership roles within the parish. Talk to them and listen to their stories. You might find exactly who you are looking for hiding right underneath your nose.

Finally, leaders who can serve as connectors have a high degree of understanding about how the Lord has gifted and called them to service. It may be that self-understanding has come naturally over many years. It could be a product of trial and error through parenting or professional life. That type of self-awareness can often be accelerated by assessment tools which provide people with an understanding of the gifts they bring as a leader. Regardless of how self-awareness developed, most connectors know how the Lord likes to use them to help others on the journey.

Dispelling Misconceptions

As we close this chapter, there are several misconceptions specific to the connected element of a clear path that should be addressed.

Not an Assembly Line

A clear path of discipleship is not an impersonal assembly line for making disciples. We are right to reject the notion that evangelization could happen in an impersonal way, with cookie-cutter programs, and along a pre-determined timeline. The connection and accompaniment provided by a clear path keeps it from becoming an impersonal assembly line.

Building a clear path does not mean just stringing together four silver bullet programs. Rather, it is a commitment to providing a context for accompanying people at every part of their journey, *no matter how long it takes an individual.* The key is for mature parish leaders (connectors) to accompany individuals from one step to the next *when the individual is ready*, not on some pre-determined timeline. Remember, it is the Holy Spirit who is ultimately leading individuals on their journey.

Again, the process of Christian initiation where adults enter the Catholic Church gives us a view to the deeply relational way the process of evangelization is supposed to unfold. Everyone who seeks to become Catholic needs a sponsor. That sponsor is supposed to be a companion throughout the journey. They are a relational bridge as individuals move from one threshold of their journey to another. A clear path of discipleship will always have people who accompany and connect with others along the journey.

Not Missing Mercy

A clear path of discipleship does not forget the corporal works of mercy. It is possible to accidentally define the mission to make disciples in such a narrow way as to exclude the corporal works of mercy. While it is true that evangelization is often associated more with the spiritual works of mercy, the corporal works often pave the way for the reception of the gospel. The corporal works of mercy help to restore credibility when the Church is perceived as an antiquated self-serving club. They also open our hearts to Jesus hidden in the distressing disguise of those in need. There is something powerful about the way service to the materially poor brings us outside of ourselves. Service to the poor cultivates freedom for experiencing ordinary spiritual conversations that we might otherwise avoid.

The Holy Spirit is always leading us to serve the materially poor in some way, shape, or form. A clear path helps develop and mature that call. In faith formation, a disciple learns about and begins to practice the corporal works of mercy. In evangelization formation, a disciple discerns his personal call, and for some that could include a particular call to an apostolate helping those in need.

A clear path equips disciples for both the spiritual and corporal works of mercy. We often separate the corporal and spiritual works of mercy. A clear path of discipleship helps us keep them connected as we make and mature disciples.

The Honest Challenge

At this point, maybe you are thinking, "This is never going to work. There is just nobody in our parish who fits the description of a connector." That is fair. Parishes without some level of evangelization formation might struggle to find leaders who can lead evangelization efforts and serve as connectors. This challenge cannot be dismissed.

There is hope, however. If the Lord has inspired in you a desire to renew your parish with a clear path of discipleship, do you think he intends for you to do so alone? The Lord always sends out laborers two by two. He calls us together in community, and he sends us out in community. Ask him. Beg him to reveal to you who he is providing as a laborer to join you.

You should expect that the leaders he provides may not be fully mature connectors yet. It is just like Christmas morning. That toy you always wanted needs to be unwrapped. It needs to be assembled. You may need to borrow batteries from the TV remote to get it started. You should expect the people sent by the Lord will not be perfect or complete leaders. After all, neither are you.

The Lord will send you companions for the journey. Your reception of them and your commitment to learn and grow together will be essential. Likely, you will have something they need for further growth and maturity as a missionary disciple. Unquestionably, they will have something you need for your own growth and maturity. The Lord will disciple you together as a community of missionary disciples along the way.

A Culture of Invitation

Knowing how to make a good invitation is somewhat of a lost art in today's world. The ease of communication provided by email, social media, and other forms of technology have confused our understanding of invitation. They have created the illusion that we are providing invitations when, in fact, we are only providing information.

Previously I provided an example of how to make an invitation to someone to serve as a connector. All good invitations have several elements, such as an illustration of the need and an explicit call to serve. The most essential element of a good invitation, however, is that it is personal. That personal element begins with how the invitation is made (e.g., a phone call versus an email). To be truly personal, however, an invitation must go beyond the manner in which it is made. It must recognize and address the recipient as an individual. That type of noticing is almost always a fruit of relationship and prayer on the part of the leader making the invitation.

The development of specific individuals as connectors will help foster a general culture of invitation in your parish. That culture will be a powerful aid in helping individuals grow and move to their next steps along your clear path.

As we move into Part II on how to build a clear path, I encourage you to intersperse your reading with the case study in Part III. The narrative in this section is the combination of dozens of real stories and instances into one fictional example.

As we begin to talk explicitly about how to build a clear path, the case study will help you see the concept and the process of building it in action.

Questions for Reflection

1. How can the ministry steps of a clear path be connected?

2. What are characteristics of a leader who serves as a "connector?"

3. Who are the individuals who already tend to serve as connectors within your parish?

4. Where can a parish or ministry find people to serve as connectors?

5. How do connectors help ensure that people can move at their own pace?

6. How are the corporal and spiritual works of mercy connected in a clear path of discipleship?

Part II
The Phases of Building a Clear Path

Introduction to Building a Clear Path

Knowing what a clear path of discipleship is and knowing how to build it are two different matters. Building a clear path of discipleship can present some unique challenges and opportunities for parish leadership. In this second part, I will lay out a systematic process for building a clear path in your parish or ministry.

I refer to the sequence of activities in building a clear path as phases because the distinction between them can sometimes be blurry. Sometimes they overlap or happen at the same time.

Despite not fitting into neat clean boxes, the process of building a clear path does follow a logical sequence. The phases build on one another. It is important to fully attend to each phase before moving on to another phase. That attention can make all the difference in building a fully functional clear path of discipleship.

Phase 1: Assessment – What is the purpose of our current ministries?

Phase 2: Discernment – What is our process for making missionary disciples?

Phase 3: Implementation – What part of the path do we build first?

Phase 4: Communication – Who needs to know what we have decided? How do we tell them?

Phase 5: Alignment – How do existing ministries connect with our clear path?

Phase 6: Expansion – What is the next step to build or expand?

Before we dive into the phases, I need to offer two disclaimers.

First, do not expect this to be a quick, effortless process. You cannot just sketch a clear path of discipleship on the back of a napkin over lunch. It is *not* just about the implementation of programs. It involves a significant cultural shift, and that will take time. Shifting culture is among the most challenging of all the various responsibilities pastors and parish leaders face. The following phases will help you build with wisdom and patience.

Second, do not try this alone. Shifting culture may begin with a small group of committed disciples who labor together under a vision from the Lord. However, if it remains only a small group, the vision will never come to complete fruition. You will need more than a handful of good people to assist you. You will, in time, need to mobilize significant portions of the entire community. More than that, however, you will need to rely on the leadership and strength of the Holy Spirit.

The Holy Spirit will be your co-laborer through the work of building a clear path. The Holy Spirit is the one who has fostered the awareness and the desire to set out on this journey. He will be the one to provide you with companions for the journey. He will ultimately be the one to provide you with the understanding and wisdom needed to navigate resistance, setbacks, and discouragement.

As you begin the process of building your clear path, I urge you to rely on the Holy Spirit as your teacher and your guide.

Chapter 6
Phase 1: Assessment

What is the purpose of our current ministries?

The assessment phase is about laying a foundation for change by gathering a small number of key parish leaders to cast a vision and assess the current reality. In the assessment phase, parish leaders ask questions, such as: What is the purpose of our current ministries? How do they connect? Where are the gaps? (To see an example of the assessment phase, reference the case study in Part III, beginning on page 166.)

Assessment Step 1: Get a Vision for Change

The first step in the process of assessment is actually to become comfortable with change. Change is hard. It is hard even when you want to do it and when you have a burning passion to change. It is almost impossible when you find yourself conflicted about the need to change. You must be free from false guilt about change. You must be free from loyalty to outmoded ways of doing things. The key to the assessment phase is having a deep conviction of the need for change. And the first step to developing conviction about the need to change is to start with a vision.

Now, some of you may be starting to get uncomfortable again because you do not think of yourselves as visionaries. Relax. Having a vision is essential. Being a visionary is not. A vision is simply a preferred picture of the future. It should excite passion and give energy, but it does not have to come from you. To be clear, you must own the vision, and it must inspire you, but you can receive a vision. You do not have to be the visionary.

There are countless places you can go to find a vision. The writings of recent popes and other authors that talk about parish renewal are a wonderful place to start. Invite others into the conversation and notice what seems to be a source of common passion. Take that passion to prayer, both individually and as a group. Let the Lord grow and deepen your passion, and do not get tripped up by trying to write a vision statement prematurely. A written vision statement can come later. Begin by finding a vision that elicits passion.

The struggle to express your vision in a neat, polite statement can indicate your team is on the right track. Holy dissatisfaction with the status quo is not a bad place to begin. One of my favorite stories of parish renewal involves a pastor and his team's early expression of their vision. They would repeat this simple rallying cry to each other: *"We are not going to be another dying church!"*

Yikes. That may seem too negative. It certainly isn't the type of thing you put on letterhead or frame for the entryway. That is the point. While this rallying cry was not pretty, it symbolized their passion, and it helped stoke their desire for change as they started on the journey.

Desire for change is the key and must be greater than the fear of change. The desire to build a clear path will help you redefine change from something to be feared to the vehicle that brings about the preferred future. Once you and your team begin to recognize change as a vehicle for that preferred future, you are ready to begin assessment.

Assessment Step 2: Lay the Foundation

Anyone helping the pastor assess the current ministries and programs of the parish will need a foundational understanding of the process of evangelization. As I mentioned earlier, there is a fun and interactive game available at clearpathbook.com under the website's Resources tab. The game can help you lay a foundational understanding of the process of conversion and discipleship for your leaders.

Regardless of how you choose to share the process of evangelization, those participating in the assessment phase will need a common understanding and language of the thresholds and the four ministry steps (Relational Outreach, Conversion Moment, Faith Formation, and Evangelization Formation) that make up a clear path. Refer to Appendices I and II. The effort you spend forming people in the foundational concepts of a clear path will continue to bear fruit as the process moves from assessment to discernment through implementation and beyond.

Assessment Step 3: Ministry Mapping

What is a ministry?

Let me start with a brief definition of ministry. Although we often speak of ministries in a variety of ways, they technically flow from the ministerial priesthood. This is different than the personal mission of all believers flowing from baptism. This baptismal mission is called an apostolate, and it is often applied outside the organizational bounds of the parish. In contrast, ministries within a parish flow from the pastor's ordination and commission. Even when they are delegated to well-formed lay men and women, those ministries are connected to his priestly ministry.[19]

The healthy relationship between parish-based ministry and personal apostolate is foundational to developing a clear path. The case study in Part III shows an example of a healthy relationship between parish-based ministry and the personal apostolate of faithful missionary disciples who want to share their faith. In a healthy parish, leaders support rather than control the expression of personal apostolates. For now, as we examine parish-based ministries, I want you to understand that

---

[19] For more on the relationship between ministry and apostolate see: Peter Andrastek, "Where Does the Ministry End and the Apostolate Begin," *Church Life Journal,* A Journal of the McGrath Institute for Church Life, April 20, 2018, online at https://churchlifejournal.nd.edu/articles/where-does-the-ministry-end-and-the-apostolate-begin/, as of June 25, 2023.

the term *ministry* provides a broad umbrella for activities and programs that make up parish life.

Ministries can, and often do, make use of a variety of programs, events, and activities for one unified goal. Youth ministry is a great example. Youth ministry often utilizes many programs to provide content and help young people grow as disciples. They also use events, such as retreats, classes, and special rites of passage. All these programs, events, and activities are part of the one ministry.

The Ministry Mapping Exercise

One practical, concrete way to assess the parish's ministries, programs, and activities is to gather a group of seven to 10 trusted parish leaders. The number of parish leaders you invite depends on the size of your parish and the number of ministries to be assessed. Most importantly, I recommend you choose mature individuals who have some prior knowledge of the thresholds of conversion and discipleship. Some awareness of the concepts behind a clear path of discipleship would also be beneficial. Set aside three hours for the initial assessment meeting, and bring plenty of snacks.

Prior to the gathering, compile a list of all the ministries and activities currently offered within your parish. Print or write each ministry on its own large index card. Next, create three 8" x 11" labels: one for the thresholds of conversion (Trust, Openness, and Seeking), one for decision (Decision), and one for the thresholds of discipleship (Beginning, Missionary, and Fruitful Disciples). Then make similar 8" x 11" labels for broad categories like "Leadership and Maintenance," "Corporal Works of Mercy," "Social Events," and "Liturgy and Devotions."

Begin by posting the thresholds of conversion and discipleship labels along a large wall, approximately 10' long. Then, post the labels with categories for other parish activities, such as "Leadership and Maintenance," on an adjacent wall. The individual ministry cards are reserved for the meeting itself. Please see the "Ministry Mapping" image as you set up this exercise.

At the start of the meeting, divide meeting participants into groups of three or four people, and hand each group a small pile of ministry cards. Ask each group to process their stack of cards by asking the question: *"Which threshold of a disciple's journey is this ministry designed to serve?"*

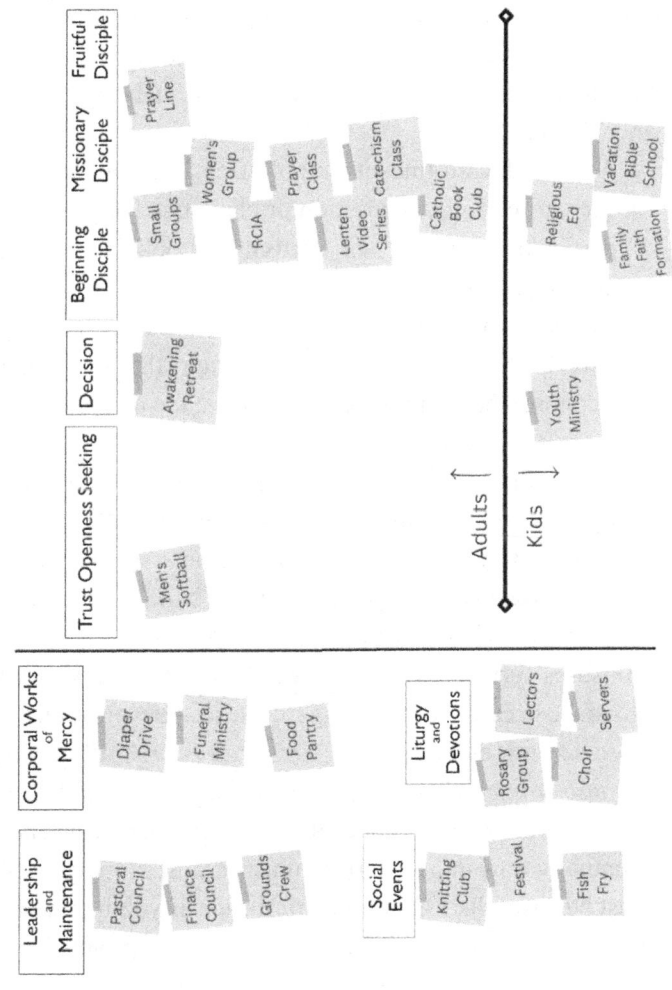

Once they answer this question for each card, coach the groups to place the card on the wall under the appropriate threshold, such as "Seeking" or "Decision."

Some cards will have ministries and activities that do not naturally fit under the thresholds of conversion and discipleship. These activities should be placed on the adjacent wall under one of the other categories, such as "Leadership and Maintenance" or "Social Events." Typically, a significant number of ministry cards will end up in these other categories.

Groups should repeat this two-step process for every parish activity and ministry. Again, if a ministry does not serve a particular threshold, place the card off the map under one of the other categories on the adjacent wall, such as "Leadership and Maintenance."

After each card finds its initial place, allow an opportunity for the entire group to question or challenge the placement of a particular ministry or activity. Look for overlaps, redundancy, and big gaps.

Notice which existing ministries serve adults and effectively help people move through the thresholds of conversion. These ministries might have the potential to serve as a step on the clear path of discipleship.

You will likely notice big gaps between ministries that serve some of the thresholds. Those gaps make it hard for individuals to grow and mature to the next step. This will be helpful to remember as you continue to build a clear path.

Finally, review your resulting map to sort programs and ministries serving children or teens and those serving adults. Move those cards representing ministries serving adults above those serving children/teens. *This step is crucially important because a parish's clear path of discipleship must focus on adults.* Although the concept of a clear path can and will eventually flow into all parish ministries, the primary emphasis must be on adults. Other ministries, such as youth ministry and religious education, will mirror the clear path you build for adults. In this way, all ministries of the parish reinforce and support each other in making disciples.

The Primacy of Adults

There are several reasons for placing a priority on adults. First, for you obedient types, this is what the bishops and popes have consistently asked from parish leaders.[20] Not surprisingly, sociological research also confirms that the faith of parents and adults is by far the most important factor influencing the faith of young people.[21] Finally, by prioritizing the development of a clear path of discipleship for adults, you ensure that the adults, who will serve the teens, have something to offer.

Youth programming that simply offers "fun" or a bland imitation of the culture usually fails to connect with young people. Young people are very astute at noticing when adults have a sincere and personal interest in them. Young people need the help of adults with a mature and vibrant faith to navigate the pressures of today's world. When teens witness that kind of attractive faith, they come, even if the adult leaders are not "cool."

In Part III's case study, you will see an example of how the renewal of the youth religious education program helped St. Mary's Parish gain access to adults they could not reach any other way. The decision to leverage the love parents have for their children is a wise strategy to reach busy millennials, but the emphasis is on the formation of adults. Quality religious education is just the means for making the connection with parents.

---

[20] Pope John Paul II, *Catechesis in Our Time*, 1979, #43. © Dicastero per la Comunicazione-Libreria Editrice Vaticana.

[21] See Dr. Christian Smith and Justin Bartkus, *"A Report on American Catholic Religious Parenting"* online at churchlife-info.nd.edu/a-report-on-american-catholic-religious-parenting as of June 27, 2023.

Much later, you can repeat the ministry mapping process for an individual ministry. To prepare for mapping a single ministry, look at how specific moments within the ministry work together to make disciples at each threshold of conversion and discipleship. You might ask yourself how new people get connected. Is it truly relational outreach or is it an impersonal sign-up in the back of church? Where is the gospel proclaimed in a conversion moment? How are the individuals formed in habits for a life of discipleship, both head and heart? Finally, where are they equipped and sent on mission? Being sent on mission cannot simply be an annual mission trip, although it might be helpful. How are people being equipped for their mission to evangelize within their lives here and now?

Whether you are doing a parish-wide assessment or mapping a single ministry, the process and questions will be the same.

Ministry Mapping: What to Expect, Pitfalls to Avoid

Expect that this process will be challenging. As Catholics, we are not accustomed to thinking about ministries within the threshold framework. That is okay. Give leaders latitude to place ministries between two thresholds because a particular ministry may indeed serve multiple thresholds.

Typically, parishes find they have many activities in the leadership and maintenance categories. Things like the Pastoral Council, the grounds crew, and the Finance Council all end up in categories off the map of the thresholds. This is good and natural. Please continue managing the finances and cutting the grass. Just avoid mistaking these activities as part of a clear path of discipleship.

Many parishes also offer many options for faith formation. Bible studies, prayer classes, and a subscription to Formed.org are just a few examples. More vibrant parishes tend to have a retreat or program that provides a conversion moment for adults. It is rare, however, for a parish to have a genuine and robust ministry designed for relational outreach or for evangelization formation. Expect to have significant gaps in ministries designed to serve the very early thresholds of conversion and the later thresholds of discipleship.

There will be a strong temptation to categorize any existing ministry with some level of hospitality or community building as relational outreach. Relational outreach is, by its definition, more than simply welcoming those who come to us. It involves *outreach* – that is, *going out*. Outreach involves intentional seeking and inviting non-members, even if the invitation includes an event on church property.

In addition to asking the question about who the ministry is designed to serve, it can also be helpful to ask the question: *Does this ministry typically move people further along the thresholds?* That question can help illustrate the difference between ministries with potential and those currently helping people grow and mature in their faith journey.

People often begin to recognize the potential for existing ministries and programs to engage individuals more deeply in the life of the parish. This is a good sign. It can also be a pitfall since future potential and current reality are not the same thing. Some ministries and programs genuinely have the potential to become an important part of a clear path of discipleship. A fish fry, for example, could be more than simply a social occasion and money-making event. A fish fry could become a method of outreach if there were an intentional effort to meet and relationally engage all the new people who come to it. However, it is crucially important to not let the potential distract from the current reality. The question really becomes: *Who is this ministry designed to serve?*

In similar fashion, there is also a temptation to get distracted discussing the effectiveness of a particular ministry. Religious education is a classic example. Most religious education programs are designed to provide faith formation for young people. Religious education assumes those young people are disciples, and it is designed to provide information and training in the life of a disciple. The problem is that our efforts sometimes fail to engage the hearts and minds of young people. Sometimes it is because the lessons are boring. Sometimes it is because the young people present are not really disciples. While it would be tempting to discuss the effectiveness of the religious education program and the real state of the hearts and minds of young people, this is not the purpose of assessment in the ministry mapping exercise.

A Word about the Mass

It can be puzzling for a parish to recognize the role of the Mass in relation to their clear path. This is ironic since the Mass is by far the most familiar activity of parish life. It is worth spending a moment to consider the relationship of the Mass to the clear path.

The Second Vatican Council referred to the Mass as the source and summit of our lives as missionary disciples,[22] but where might it belong on the clear path? Does it belong on the clear path? Attempting to categorize the Mass as one of the steps on the clear path may feel a little odd. Where should you put the meeting of heaven and earth in the process of conversion and discipleship? A couple of considerations might help.

Let us return to Pope Saint Paul VI. In the document where he spoke about evangelization as the deepest identity of the Church, he also gave a quick synopsis of what evangelization entails.

"Evangelizing is in fact the grace and vocation proper to the Church, her deepest identity. She exists in order to evangelize, that is to say, in order to preach and teach, to be the channel of the gift of grace, to reconcile sinners with God,

---

[22] Second Vatican Council, *Constitution on the Sacred Liturgy*, 1963, #10. © Dicastero per la Comunicazione-Libreria Editrice Vaticana.

and to perpetuate Christ's sacrifice in the Mass, which is the memorial of His death and glorious resurrection."[23]

Note how the Mass is not just listed as part of evangelization, but so many of the moments of evangelization like preaching, teaching, the giving of grace, and the reconciliation of sinners, happen at Mass. The Mass is a special renewal of all these moments of evangelization.

In many ways Pope Saint Paul VI was just building on the teaching of Vatican II. Ten years earlier, the Council noted the Mass was the source and summit of our lives as disciples. It also noted that the Mass is not the *entirety* of our Christian lives. The Council said Mass must be *preceded* by evangelization and formation and followed by service in the world.[24]

This makes sense when we remember the necessary preparation for our First Holy Communion, one of our sacraments of initiation. The Mass is, by design, an event for insiders. It requires initiation and formation. Have you ever tried to bring a non-Catholic or a non-Christian to Mass? If you have, you know it requires more than a little explanation. From this perspective, we can see that the Mass is clearly designed for disciples. Remember the design question: Who is this ministry designed to serve? The Mass is designed for disciples to gather in communal worship. It assumes a decision for Jesus and a substantial amount of faith formation.

At this point you might be thinking that hospitality and welcoming people back to Mass are often the first steps for a parish to become more missional. In some ways you are correct, but that is because the first step to becoming a missional community is often recognizing the current community. This includes people already in the pews. Whether they attend Mass regularly or not, they are essential parts of

---

[23] Pope Paul VI, *Evangelization in the Modern World*, 1975, #14. © Dicastero per la Comunicazione-Libreria Editrice Vaticana.

[24] Second Vatican Council, *Constitution on the Sacred Liturgy*, 1963, #9. © Dicastero per la Comunicazione-Libreria Editrice Vaticana.

community building. Even more, the Mass is sometimes one of the first places fallen-away Catholics re-encounter the Lord and their parish community. All this reinforces the fact that the Mass is designed for disciples, even if they have been away for a while.

If we go too far in trying to make the Mass hospitable to outsiders, we risk emptying the Mass of its unique meaning as a gathering of disciples. Please be hospitable to newcomers who join your community for worship at Mass, but remember the Mass requires initiation. It is okay that the Mass is designed for those who have been initiated. It is likely that many who are present may need a renewed encounter and personal conversion. A beautiful liturgy may help spark that encounter. Just do not expect the Mass to provide your primary conversion moment. More than likely, other specifically designed ministries will be needed to foster conversion.

As the source and summit of our lives as missionary disciples, the Mass is our weekly gathering with other missionaries to be renewed and strengthened for the week ahead. We are reminded of the truth we proclaim, strengthened with the Eucharist, and then sent out for another week. In this sense, the Mass could be understood as a continual conversion moment, as well as a type of faith formation and even evangelization formation.

In non-Catholic churches, a conversion moment is occasionally referred to as an "altar call." Once the preacher has finished proclaiming the gospel, people are invited to come forward to the altar to pray and give their lives to Christ. If we have eyes to see it, the Mass is the ultimate altar call for those of us who are already disciples. Each week, after hearing the Word of God proclaimed, we come forward to offer ourselves again to the Lord. We receive him as our Lord and Savior – not just in our hearts but into our bodies.

Ultimately, I believe the Mass stands above the clear path, deepening the graces initially experienced by people in their conversion and formation as missionary disciples. To understand the place of the Mass, we must respect its design. The Mass is a gift given to us, which we must receive with reverence. Our efforts to make the Mass more hospitable, engaging, and beautiful must all respect the design given to us by the universal Church. Part of the genius of building a clear path of discipleship is that we have the freedom to let the Mass be the Mass. We have no need to force it to be something it is not. Instead, we surround it with evangelization and formation so it can truly be the source and summit it was designed to be.

Questions for Reflection

1. Why is it important that a parish's clear path focus on adults?

2. Apart from a formal mission statement, what is your vision or dream for your parish?

3. What is the Mass designed to do? How can a clear path help us respect that design?

4. Where do you think there might be gaps in your parish's existing ministries that serve as the steps of a clear path of discipleship?

5. Where might there be duplicated efforts in your parish's ministries and programs?

6. How well do you think the current ministries and programs in your parish work together to make disciples? Why?

Chapter 7
Phase 2: Discernment

What is our process for making missionary disciples?

The discernment phase of building a clear path of discipleship is about developing a blueprint for the future ministries that will make up the clear path. It relies upon your formal assessment of the ministries that exist and the gaps you identified in your mapping exercise during the assessment phase. You will begin to discern which gaps the Lord is calling you to fill and how.

The discernment phase also relies on a clear picture of your mission field and your vision for mature disciples. Your blueprint will represent the tangible fruit of your discernment, and it will end up guiding your ongoing efforts to build a clear path. (To see an example of the discernment phase, reference the case study in Part III beginning on page 171.)

Discernment as Prayer, Thought, and Action

Your discernment will involve a dynamic cycle of three elements: prayer, thought, and action. Good discernment involves all three elements unfolding together. Sometimes one or more of the elements will dominate a season or moment of discernment, but ideally, they will all be present together, even if they are not formally distinguished.

The prayer element will be an intentional listening to the Lord. You are asking for his direction and guidance as to what your clear path should look like. This prayer should be a communal experience, which gives space for a select group of leaders to come together in seeking the Lord's guidance. This can happen for a few minutes at a standing meeting, for a few hours at a special gathering, or for a full day at a leadership retreat. You must also find a way to make regular time for prayer as part of your ongoing discernment.

One simple tool for this communal prayer is the discernment rosary. It is a simple and familiar way for a group of people to bring specific questions of discernment to the Lord. This simple practice provides a method for a group of leaders to concretely seek the Lord's guidance in prayer together. Appendices III and IV include a full explanation of the discernment rosary. A list of principles for group discernment is located at the end of this chapter.

Our prayer will naturally be intertwined with our thoughts about what a clear path might look like in our context. The thinking element of discernment will likely involve research into potential programs for a ministry step on the clear path. It will likely involve questions around the health and fruitfulness of current ministries. Conversation and discussion will be key to this thinking as it is unlikely one person has all the information necessary for a fully informed decision.

Like prayer, designating time for thinking and conversation is essential to good discernment. Most people hesitate to dive into the type of thinking discernment requires without a time clearly set aside for that purpose. Since so much of our meetings are dedicated to setting a course for immediate action, people need permission and a separate gathering to ask big open-ended questions, such as: What does a mature missionary disciple look like in our parish?

Finally, good discernment also involves action. The action element of discernment may include simple actions, such as research or a conversation with a key leader. It will eventually involve taking concrete steps to build a ministry step on the clear path. Those actions will be infused with prayer and thinking, but it is helpful to consider the actions themselves as a part of the discernment process. In my experience, the Lord likes to provide clarity, but not *certainty*. That is, we know our next steps with clarity, but we still need to step out in faith without the certainty that things will unfold as we imagine. It is often through our actions that we recognize more fully what the Lord has in mind for us and find confirmation in our discernment process.

Discernment will be a cycle of prayer, thought, and action flowing through the discernment phase and the entirety of your efforts to build a clear path.

Discernment Step 1: Develop a Picture of Your Mission Field

The first task in discernment is to again gather a select group of leaders to pray and to think through the mission field in which your parish will seek to make disciples. This group does not need to be a cross-section of the parish. As might be expected, individuals who participated in the assessment process will be extremely helpful. They have the context for discernment. Also, key to this step are individuals for whom prayer is an established way of life. These are people whose mature prayer life makes them comfortable recognizing the Lord's voice. Again, you will rely upon individuals who understand the process of evangelization. Individuals who have been deeply formed in the process of evangelization will be key to every phase of building a clear path.

By mission field, I mean the people within the territorial boundaries and sphere of influence of your parish. This is essential because too often we begin our efforts to build a clear path by looking inward. It can be extremely easy to build a clear path that makes our parish more comfortable for us. That is not what it means to be a missional community. We must begin by directing our eyes outward to the people our parish feels called to make disciples. What are the hopes, dreams, fears, and challenges of the people that your parish community or ministry serves?

To this end, you may want to consult with a local demographer to get a picture of the makeup of your local community. The demographic landscape of our communities can be surprising to us. We all have routines and rhythms of life that can blind us to changes in our neighborhoods and towns. Those changes happen over time. Unless we pay close attention, we can easily find ourselves trying to serve in ways that no longer suit our mission field.

One of my favorite examples comes from St. Francis Cabrini Parish in Omaha, Nebraska. As one of the oldest parishes in the city, they have a long history of serving Italian immigrants, but almost all the Italian immigrants and their children moved away decades ago. Today the neighborhood is a hip and trendy millennial center. In the words of the pastor, "Until we faced the reality that we had a new mission field and changed our methods, we were never going to reach that mission field."

The key to executing this first step is to discern who the parish is *uniquely* called to serve. Notice the type of people the Lord seems to be bringing to mind. Who is he putting on your heart, and how is God inviting you to reach that person? How does this person think about church? What is his or her background? What are the obstacles that inhibit his or her encounter with Jesus and his or her growth as a disciple? What are his or her needs? The people and their accompanying needs will be numerous. Just remember to distinguish between a need and a call. Not every unmet need is a call from the Lord.

You may want to give this personalized image of your mission field a nickname. You can refer to this character's needs and desires in your ongoing discernment and planning. With this character image at the forefront, slowly but surely you will begin to see the next steps for making disciples of the actual people the Lord has placed on your heart.

Discernment Step 2: Develop a Picture of Mature Discipleship

Before beginning the process of discerning which step along the clear path to build and what a complete path might look like for your parish, you must begin with the end in mind. That is, you must have a clear picture of what a missionary disciple looks like in your parish. It is not about appearances.

It is about the head, heart, and habits. Develop a collection of anecdotes. What does a missionary disciple sound like in conversation? How does a missionary disciple behave differently than a disciple who has not yet felt a personal call to share their faith? What is the difference between someone who has heard the call to share their faith and someone who consistently and fruitfully does share their faith? What are the attitudes and behaviors that distinguish someone as a true missionary disciple?

These and other related questions will help you form an image of what a mature disciple looks like in your parish or ministry. You may want to give your ideal mature disciple a nickname as mentioned above, such as "Fruitful Frank." You will likely find a better name, but you get the point. Knowing what a mature disciple looks like and how they behave is essential. You can ask yourself questions, such as: What would Frank do? What does Frank need from this community to live as a fruitful disciple?

Perhaps most importantly, you can now ask yourself the big question: *How can our parish produce fruitful missionary disciples like Frank?* That question helps you discern the ministries that will make up your clear path.

Discernment Step 3: Develop an Initial Blueprint of Your Clear Path

The development of a blueprint for your parish's clear path is relatively simple. Again, gather your key leaders to pray through a series of questions.

- Relational Outreach – How will we relationally connect with non-practicing and non-believing members of our local community?
- Conversion Moment – How will we proclaim the gospel and foster conversion?
- Faith Formation – How will we mature new disciples?

- Evangelization Formation – How will we equip disciples for their personal mission?

The answers to these questions should be concrete ministries made up of programs, special events, and experiences that provide the context for growth along a clear path in your parish. At this point, the answers to those questions are still just a blueprint. Blueprints and plans can change, but it is never a good idea to start building without a plan.

Although the discernment of a clear path of discipleship will be unique to every parish, there are a few patterns and best practices that should be considered.

Discernment Pro Tip #1: Start by Prioritizing Adults

The most important thing to remember when developing your blueprint is to prioritize the evangelization and formation of adults. They will become the leaders who build your clear path. They will also build those ministries that mirror your clear path for specific demographics. These adults will lead and organize the outreach to teens. They will bring the gospel to life through the corporal works of mercy. They will be the leaders coordinating the basic maintenance of the parish.

It is the evangelization and formation of adults that will change the culture of your parish so every service and offering can naturally become a moment of grace. Other ministries to particular demographic groups, such as teens or children, will end up mirroring and reinforcing the clear path that focuses on adults.

Discernment Pro Tip #2: Start by Prioritizing Encounter and Conversion

If your assessment revealed a big gap in the conversion moment step, it is best to begin there. Fostering new and renewed conversion for adults tends to be the key that unlocks the development of every other step in the clear path. People who have experienced conversion desire to learn and grow as disciples. People who have had a renewed encounter are more likely to serve and seek to be equipped for evangelization. People who have had a new or renewed encounter cannot help but begin to want that encounter for others. They may need encouragement and equipping, but they *want* to reach out to those who are not connected to the community.

Discernment Pro Tip #3: Start by Listening to God, Not Reviewing Existing Programs

There can be a strong temptation to simply look at the results of your assessment phase and try to squeeze existing ministries and programs into steps on your clear path. For those of us who are conflict avoidant, our minds can quickly try to make an existing ministry work in the attempt to avoid an uncomfortable conversation. The fear that people will not like what you choose can be paralyzing. You can prevent this trap by really focusing on where the Lord is leading you. How is he asking you to make disciples? Begin with this question and let the question of how current ministries might fit into the clear path come later.

One powerful way to discern where the Lord is leading is to remember the story of your own discipleship journey. Notice the patterns of how you and members of your team grew and matured. Although we want to be careful not to project our story onto others, our own stories offer wisdom in the discernment process. Sometimes that wisdom will remind us of what to avoid. At other times, it may serve as a model to repeat. Regardless of the lesson, you can trust that your experiences and those of your team will be relevant to the discernment of your clear path.

Discernment Pro Tip #4: Start with What You Have

Even though it can be a trap to begin with current ministries, you do not have to start with a blank slate. Oftentimes, the Lord has provided an existing program or ministry that can serve as one of the steps of your clear path.

In Part III's case study, the St. Mary's team simply plugged into a local retreat movement as their conversion moment. Chances are there is a similar opportunity in a neighboring parish, a local movement, or a conference which can become a step on your clear path.

It is ideal for ministries of your clear path to be run by parish leaders and be tailored to the specific needs of your parish. But do not let the ideal keep you from getting started. A perfectly tailored program run by members of your parish is a lot of work. Be careful not to bite off more than you can chew. As you begin, give yourself permission to start small and use what is available. Remember, you can start with a dirt road. Notice where the Lord is already making and maturing disciples and begin to build there.

Do not despair if your head is starting to swim. The process of making disciples is integrated, so the process of building a clear path is also integrated. It can feel like the chicken or egg question. It can be tricky to know where to begin. It all fits together, and it is all interrelated.

Discernment Pro Tip #5: Start with Who You Have

The individuals the Lord has given you should also guide your discernment of what to build next. The passions and gifting of the specific individuals who are present as leaders can be a powerful discernment for your clear path. Ministries and programs do not run themselves. They are run by people. As you discern what step on the path you are called to build next, focus on the people the Lord has given you. Who has the Lord provided, and what are their passions and gifts? The people the Lord has provided as leaders will be a powerful signpost in your discernment of what step to build and when.

Guiding Principles for Group Discernment

As you begin the process of discernment about which part of the clear path to build next, it is important to keep several principles for discernment in mind.

Unity of Desire – Asking the following questions can help establish unity. Who do we have the greatest hunger to serve or equip? What is the most urgent need for the clear path? Where does the Lord seem to be drawing our hearts? It is especially important that the group does not settle for artificial unity. Everyone must have the time and space to express their ideas and desires. Give people permission to speak up. You must also patiently wait for everyone to name the desires or fears they are feeling.

Open Doors – Often the Lord has already provided what we need before we ask. What next step of building our path seems clear, simple, and easy? Where has God already provided the resources and leaders for us to move forward? Where can we make the biggest difference? Where is the Lord providing a consoling and encouraging hand in our efforts?

Missionary Hearts – Who are the people the Holy Spirit has raised up for this labor? What do their passions teach us about what is next? Pay close attention to what is in the hearts and minds of the people who will be leading the proposed initiatives.

The Spirit's Leading – Where does the Holy Spirit already seem to be at work? What seems to be happening naturally and organically within each step of the clear path, even if that is not happening in a systematic or programmatic way? If you look closely, you will see the Holy Spirit has likely made a dirt path ahead of your efforts to build a clear path. Start there and let the Spirit guide you.

Obedience – Where do the words and efforts of our ordained leaders seem to be leading? What about their words and actions seem confusing and need clarification? What more do you need to give a full and joyful yes to their invitations? If there are reservations or concerns that inhibit your ability to freely embrace what is being asked, do not fake it, just ask. Humbly inquire about what concerns you. The answers will be key to moving forward in genuine obedience.

In many ways, the work of discernment persists all the way through the building of a clear path of discipleship. Real, fruitful discernment involves prayer, thinking, and action. As you move on to implementation and building the next step of your clear path, remember to continue to pray and think even as your discernment becomes more active.

Questions for Reflection

1. What are the unique needs of your mission field?
2. What might a mature missionary disciple look like in your parish?
3. How can you tell when a group is hearing the voice of the Lord together?
4. Who comes to mind as potential leaders for ministries on the clear path?
5. What formation or training might these potential leaders need to build additional ministry steps on your clear path?

Chapter 8
Phase 3: Implementation

What part of the path do we build first?

The implementation phase is where the fruit of all previous labor begins to come to life. It is where a parish begins to take concrete steps to build or to refine a particular ministry as a step on their clear path of discipleship. Sometimes a step needs to be created entirely from scratch. Other times, an existing ministry or program can be adapted to fit the need.

Often the biggest challenge in the implementation phase is the desire to do too much too soon. Although the formal discernment of a clear path blueprint may have ended, discernment remains essential to fruitful implementation. The question of whether or not this step comes from an existing ministry or an entirely new initiative must be discerned. The pastor and his team must still discern the leaders the Lord has called. They must also discern *their* role in supporting those leaders.

Perhaps most importantly, leaders must discern the overall timeline as the tasks unfold. Implementing just one new step in a parish-wide clear path of discipleship can take six months to a year, or more. There will be a temptation to rush implementation. Please resist this temptation. The pace of implementation must allow for ongoing discernment. Discernment takes time. In the end, however, it saves far more time than it takes.

The more dramatic the cultural change for the leaders, the longer it will take. Sometimes, the plan may require additional tilling of the soil and casting vision to surface new leaders who can help in the implementation of the new or revised step on the clear path. The temptation to skip straight to the implementation of some new program will be overwhelming. Do not give in to it. The time spent casting vision and finding leaders is always worth it. (To see an example of the implementation phase, reference the case study in Part III beginning on page 177.)

Implementation Step 1: Cast Vision for *Why* Things Will Change

The first task for implementation is to provide vision for key leaders and volunteers for why things need to change. Think about it. Once you start to tell people what specifically needs to change and how things are going to be different, everyone has an opinion. Consider the fictional example of parking lot maintenance.

What – "No, let's not totally repave the parking lot. Let's just resurface it."

How – "Let's not take bids. Let's just have guys in the parish do it."

Why – "We are going to be proactive with our facility maintenance so we can be good stewards of our resources and save money in the long-run."

Notice how the *why* of our fictional parking lot project unites. Generally, nobody wants to argue about good maintenance and stewardship. So too, as you begin to articulate the *why* of your clear path's implementation, go back to the essential mission of the Church to make disciples. The *why* of a clear path is the changed lives of our friends, family, and co-workers. Casting vision for the *why* of your implementation is your first and irreplaceable step as you get started building your clear path.

Implementation Step 2: Find the Leader(s) to Help

If the Lord is indeed calling you to do something, he is going to provide the capacity to do it. Sometimes that means a reallocation of our own time and energy. Just as often, it means inviting someone else to help.

The leaders who will help you implement a clear path may or may not have been involved in the process up to this point.

If the first few phases of building a clear path tend to be heavy on prayer, discernment, and strategic thinking, the later phases tend to be heavy on execution and communication. Of course, everyone will need the vision of why (see Step 1), but you can expect people with gifts for execution and communication to surface later in the process.

Finding leaders with these skills is again a process of that threefold discernment dynamic detailed in Chapter 7. Ask the Lord to send you help. Pray through a list of names, and then act by having a conversation with those who surfaced about why you think they can help.

Allow me to offer a word of warning: do not discern for people. Let people decide for themselves. This of course means avoiding pressure and manipulation to try to get people to help. I doubt that is your temptation.

The real temptation is to say "no" for people. The thing to remember is leaders are made to lead, and they will find a way to be busy with something. Busy people get things done, and sometimes we hesitate to ask because we know people are busy. Great leaders want to be part of great projects. Why not invite them into the salvation of souls?

Implementation Step 3: Develop a Plan

Too often we set out to start some new initiative without taking stock of what is necessary to accomplish it. This is human nature, but Jesus warns us to think through the cost (Lk. 14:28ff). Implementation needs a plan. A goal without a plan is just a wish. Even with a good plan, it can still be challenging to implement new ideas. Without a plan, there is almost no chance you will be able to build your clear path.

The tasks, timeline, and individuals responsible for making things happen must be clearly known by all involved. A simple implementation plan will help keep leaders with vision grounded for their next steps. A simple plan at the beginning of implementation will tell leaders with a natural gifting for execution that you are serious. An implementation plan will ensure that your blueprint begins to come to life in a timely manner.

In Appendices VI and VII, you will find a simple template for making an implementation plan called the Clear Objectives Worksheet. This worksheet will help you develop a handful of goals, as well as determine who will complete which tasks and by what date. A few actionable goals are crucial to focusing you and your team's attention during the implementation phase. The worksheet also provides a simple way to share those goals to keep people focused and accountable.

Implementation Pro Tip #1: Expect to Equip and Train Leaders

Building any new ministry along the clear path will require leaders. Those leaders will need a bit of encouragement, direction, and formation to get started. They will need to be equipped for the ministry you are inviting them to help establish. In this sense, you might think of your first step as evangelization formation. You will likely need to do some formation of leaders who build and coordinate your conversion moment. This type of equipping of leaders will be simple. Many programs offer short videos and start-up guides that provide a good initial formation for leaders. Over time, you may want to consider conferences and additional options for formation. Do not worry. If you keep listening, your leaders will tell you how they need to be equipped for ongoing mission.

Implementation Pro Tip #2: Wait to Broadly Communicate Your Clear Path

By this phase of the process, you may be excited to tell the wider parish community about your plans to build a clear path of discipleship. Wait. The work of communication and alignment will require change. It is extremely helpful to have momentum and proof of concept as you begin to communicate more broadly. It is much easier to shift attention and resources when real fruit has already begun to appear. Let the fruit speak for itself. The time will come for broader communication. For now, focus on building a step on your clear path and changing lives.

Consider this implementation phase like the silent phase of a capital campaign. You have been hard at work discerning and now building the first steps on your clear path. When the time comes to communicate more broadly, you will have stories to tell and real momentum to invite people to join.

Implementation Pro Tip #3: Distinguish Between Types of Ministries

After developing a blueprint for your clear path, it may also be helpful to review your ministry map from the assessment phase and distinguish between various types of ministries. This distinction will be key to helping you recognize how ministries fit together as you start to build. This understanding will also be helpful as you move into the alignment and communication phases.

There are at least three different distinctions I recommend making: 1. Clear path ministries; 2. Parish sponsored ministries; and 3. All other activities. The work done through Ministry Mapping, as detailed in Chapter 6, has begun this process. This distinction will help you give the best of your time and energy to ministries that most directly contribute to the making and maturing of disciples.

First, you will want to distinguish certain ministries as *clear path ministries*. These ministries are clearly designed to further an individual's faith journey through a specific threshold of the conversion or discipleship process. An example would be a retreat that provides the primary conversion moment on the parish clear path. These ministries will take priority in scheduling, promotion, and in developing leaders. They are elevated, in a sense, because of the responsibility they carry to assist people's growth in their faith journey.

That does not mean, however, that there is no room for other ministries or programs. The presence of other ministries can also aid people's growth, even if they are not designated as part of the clear path.

The second distinction identifies *parish sponsored ministries* not on the clear path. Something like the parish sponsored theology night might be an example. Unless the theology night becomes a specific step on the clear path, it will not be as prominently promoted or directly supported by parish leadership. A ministry can still be helpful to the overall mission, even if it is not part of the clear path.

One of the most important ways a ministry, not part of the clear path, can be helpful is by connecting people with ministries that are on the clear path. Again, you can think of them like on-ramps and side streets. As long as these ministries connect back to the clear path at some point, they can make a significant contribution to the overall effort to make and mature disciples.

Finally, it is helpful to recognize that not every activity needs to be categorized as part of the clear path or as a parish sponsored ministry. There are some *other activities* that might be beneficial but are not really ministries. Scouting clubs and the grounds crew are examples of this category. Again, these activities have value. Their connection to the main mission of making disciples is more peripheral, and for this reason, they should not take priority for facility reservations, promotion in the bulletin, or support from key leaders.

For parishes that receive frequent requests for facility rental, you might want to add a fourth category for *non-parish activities*. Remember, just because an activity involves people from your parish does not mean it is a ministry or a parish sponsored activity. You may choose to charge a fee to groups that rent parish facilities.

If applying this distinction seems like it will be hard in practice, remember the importance of clarity. The most important thing about categorizing ministries is providing clarity for leaders about what is most important. If everything is important, then nothing is important. While it is true that this distinction between various types of ministries and activities might be hard for some people to receive, it is essential for the development of a clear path. Making clear distinctions now will help avoid confusion and conflict later.

Implementation Pro Tip #4: Fail Small and Fast

One of the keys to executing change well is to begin with small, short experiments. Let the good grow, and then reproduce it. Learn from your mistakes and adjust. Even a well-researched and discerned plan for a new ministry or program for your clear path may not work. Even if it does work, you are guaranteed a few hiccups and missteps along the way. You can minimize their negative effects by trying new ideas in small and short experiments.

One example of a small, short experiment is implementing a conversion moment retreat. You could also attend another parish's retreat or hold one at your parish for a few chosen participants who best reflect your target audience. Another example is to ask one existing small group to try a new method of prayer or new small group material for a few weeks instead of asking everyone to try it for a full year. You could test a new evangelization formation idea on a few people before adding it to an existing program. You get the idea. Commit to trying things in small settings over short periods of time. If it fails, you fail small and fast. What you learn will ultimately give you confidence for the growth and expansion you desire.

Implementation Pro Tip #5: Wait on Relational Outreach

Relational outreach is crucial to building a clear path. It helps the disciples in your parish share their faith outside the parish community. Outreach must always be present, but a formal relational outreach ministry is rarely the place to start. Relational outreach is often the first sequential step that non-members take, but it is usually the last step to be built. This might be surprising but think about what relational outreach requires. The relational outreach ministry requires leaders who are equipped to be missionary disciples. Before you can start outreach, those leaders must first be formed for going out. Begin by converting hearts within the community with a conversion moment ministry. Next, form those disciples and equip them as missionaries. Once you have enough disciples equipped to share their faith in a relational way, your relational outreach can take off.

There is another reason to wait to build your relational outreach step. For better or for worse, a formal relational outreach step will reflect the larger parish culture. If your parish is still struggling with hospitality, it will show in your relational outreach. More importantly, if your parish is not consistently changing lives with the gospel, your relational outreach will lack the communal witness of committed disciples. The witness of the community must compliment and confirm the witness of the mature missionary disciples who have built trust with non-believers.

Waiting on relational outreach gives time for the cultural shifts in your parish to grow so your relational outreach can really reflect the larger faith community you seek to invite others to join.

Implementation Pro Tip #6: Utilize Small Groups for Every Step of Your Clear Path

Small groups are one of the most fruitful methods of the new evangelization. They are infinitely flexible and adaptable to members' needs. They are recession-proof and pandemic-proof. For those living in countries closed to public faith gatherings, they are persecution-proof. And the best part is that small groups work for almost any step along your clear path.

Small groups can be the delivery vehicle of a ministry step, or they can be a component of any step on your path. Small groups work exceptionally well as the delivery vehicle for the faith formation step. Their flexibility allows group members to receive the content specific to their needs in the context of a prayerful community. As a component of a ministry step, they often provide a place for connection and discussion as seen during a conversion moment retreat. Evangelization formation often also has a small group component that helps provide accountability and encouragement to disciples being equipped for mission.

Finally, small groups can provide a non-threatening context for missionary disciples to invite friends and family to a first step of faith. Although the content of the small groups may vary widely depending on the step they serve, the small group method is an invaluable tool for building every step on your clear path.

Questions for Reflection:

1. How can you identify the doers, thinkers, and other roles among the individuals called to serve?
2. Who are the missionary disciples in your parish who might be capable of leading the development of a new step on your parish clear path?
3. What might those leaders need in terms of formation or encouragement?
4. Why is it important to wait for broad scale communication?
5. How can distinguishing between types of ministries be helpful for creating a clear path?
6. Why does relational outreach often develop later in the building process?
7. Why are small groups an effective method for almost every ministry step on the clear path?

Chapter 9
Phase 4: Communication

*Who needs to know what we have decided
and how do we tell them?*

The communication phase is where you go public with the communication of your plans and efforts to build a clear path. You might wonder why communication is Phase 4 of building a clear path and not much earlier in the process. After all, communication has been happening throughout the entire process. Communication must begin early and persist throughout every phase of building a clear path. Key leaders must be gathered, given a vision for the clear path, and invited to join in assessment and discernment. Their understanding and counsel are key to their buy-in and commitment.

This early communication is much like the silent phase of a fundraising campaign for a capital improvement building project. Many of the most important constituents are brought into the conversation at the very beginning. It is not until after some momentum is established that the whole parish, and even the wider community, are invited. *The communication phase is about the broad and public communication conveying what has taken place and what will happen.*

This broader communication is less conversational. It is more informative and includes an invitation. As such, it is helpful to share stories of the momentum resulting from the early efforts.

Again, like a fundraising campaign, it is helpful to have key constituents already committed and real momentum established before going public. (To see an example of the communication phase, reference the case study in Part III beginning on page 185.)

Back to the Beginning

The most essential element of the communication phase is repetition of why you are building a clear path. Although communication is clearly needed through every phase, it takes on added importance and greater visibility once there is real momentum in the building of the first new step in your clear path. Parish leaders can forget the importance of repetition in their communication. By this point in the process, they have been thinking and discussing the concepts of a clear path of discipleship for months, maybe even for years. Some people have already been brought into the process, and their reactions have helped shape the clear path's development. Chances are others, with whom the leaders frequently associate, also have an awareness of the progress in building a clear path. That does not mean, however, that everyone knows or understands.

Communication must happen in a variety of ways and, depending on the audience, at varying degrees of depth. Tools, such as social media, bulletins, and e-mails, are invaluable. They can, however, give the false impression that your communication is connecting with your audience. Repeated and consistent messaging from leaders in a face-to-face format is essential. This is because the key concepts behind a clear path of discipleship are still very new in a typical parish. If they are to communicate effectively to a wider audience, it is important for leaders to remember they need to go back to the very beginning of their clear path journey.

Communication Step 1: Form a Communication Team

It is important that all the face-to-face communication responsibilities do not land on the pastor alone. He must have the support of several leaders who can share the responsibility of communicating the vision for a clear path and listening to feedback with a discerning ear. This goes beyond individuals who can effectively use social media tools. It will again involve individuals who have joined the pastor in the assessment, discernment, and implementation phases, but now may also include those with a professional background in communications or marketing. The ideal team size will vary according to the parish's size and the community's cultural receptivity.

Adding team members with a background in marketing or communications requires special considerations. A parishioner or an outside consultant could provide this expertise. If you choose to utilize an outsider who has not participated in the assessment and discernment phases of the process, you will find both advantages and disadvantages to their lack of context. Context is helpful, but good communications and marketing professionals make it a priority to understand their client's needs and message. Context can also be as blinding as it is helpful. When we know all the backstory, we sometimes forget to tell it to others. A newcomer's professional insights may be a powerful advantage in conveying your message publicly. If you are willing to listen, outsiders may also help you identify gaps in your communication.

Communication Step 2: Develop a Communication Plan

As you begin to develop a public communication plan for your clear path, there are several essential elements that must be included.

Concentric Circles – How you communicate will vary depending on the constituency receiving your message and the time it is delivered. Each circle will encompass more people. The purpose of these three concentric circles of communication can be summarized as involve, inform, and invite.

Involve – Communication with trusted leaders, who are offering counsel on the development of the clear path, must involve them in the process. This communication is much more than interactive dialogue for the sake of discernment. This is especially true of leaders who will be invited to take an active role in the facilitation of ministries on the clear path.

Inform – Communication to the broader parish community should inform people about the development of the clear path and its ongoing implementation. The general parishioner will not offer counsel as to what ministries make up the clear path, but they should understand some of the discernment that went into its development. At a minimum, they must be informed about the ministries that make up the clear path and how to take their first step.

Invite – Communication about the clear path must come in the form of an invitation to all, not just current parishioners and insiders. At some level, communication about your clear path should be accessible to outsiders. Some of that communication will come in the form of signage and other public media. The majority will come from individuals who are part of the community and can easily invite non-members to connect. Equipping faithful members of your community to communicate a next step on the clear path represents the crowning achievement of the communication process. Can you imagine a parish community where all members quickly and easily share with non-members how to connect with your parish for a next step that fits their personal faith journey? That would be a truly missional community.

The Content – The content of your communication should always follow the pattern of sharing the purpose, the picture, the plan, and the part individuals will play in your clear path.[25]

Purpose – The purpose of your clear path is almost synonymous with the why of building a clear path. It will likely include some background information on the condition of faith engagement in your state, county, and neighborhood. It will likely also include data on attendance, giving, and entry into the Church for your parish. Just be careful to firmly root the explanation of the purpose of building a clear path in the

---

[25] The four P's model comes from *Managing Transitions (25th Anniversary Edition),* **by William Bridges and Susan Bridges, copyright © 2017. Reprinted by permission of Hachette Go, an imprint of Hachette Book Group, Inc.**

mission of the Church to make disciples and how that mission changes the lives of those we love.

WARNING: *Anything less than the mission of the Church can easily become a self-centered effort to make your parish ministry more comfortable for yourselves.* Most of your communication must center on the purpose of a clear path because that why will ultimately unite the community in its reception of the message.

Picture – The picture of the destination is a crucial and often forgotten communication step because it is usually someplace that people have never been. It can be difficult for someone to imagine something outside their experience. To help paint the picture of what is possible, tell stories of lives already changed by the ministries that make up your clear path.

Plan – Sharing the plan for your clear path will help individuals begin to conceptualize the what and how of your clear path. Sharing a verbal and visual outline of your parish's blueprint will be a crucial element of communication. The wider community may not know all the details, but they do need a general outline.

Part – Everyone needs to know their part in the clear path. Knowing their part offers people confirmation that they have a place and a sense of belonging. This sense of belonging is essential for people to withstand changes to familiar routines, structures, and programs. So often when people leave a parish, it is because they no longer know their part.

Specific roles will vary based on discernment by both parish leadership and the individual, but everyone must know where they fit. For most parishioners, their part will begin with an invitation to participate in the next step that fits their personal faith journey. The invitation need not be elaborate, but it must be present.

Methods – There are many communication methods available. A communication plan that utilizes as many methods as possible will be more effective than one that only uses a couple. This helps to ensure delivery to the broadest audience and to ensure message saturation. Here are a few methods you could utilize.

Face-to-Face – This is by far the most important means of communication for those in your parish. Although it could be impractical for everyone to have a personal face-to-face invitation, especially in a large parish, it is the most effective means of communicating something as new and important as a clear path. Seeking to use this method as far as possible is important. Take the time to brainstorm a list of key leaders and groups that need to receive the message through face-to-face communication. Prepare simple talking points and try to think ahead and prepare for frequently asked questions. Get others on board to help make these face-to-face invitations.

Homilies – Although less interactive, homilies provide a privileged place for a spiritual father to invite the worshiping community to join in the building of a clear path. Your parish's clear path must be simple enough that pastors and deacons can preach on it and summarize it quickly. When we have eyes to see it, the call to evangelization shows up everywhere in scripture. Take advantage of the cycle of readings to preach on some aspect of the clear path at least once a month. It will be more frequent at the outset, but even when the clear path is firmly established in parish culture and operations, it should remain a part of the preaching message at least once a quarter.

Social Media – Good communication provides short, repeated, and consistent messages. This is even more important when the ideas and behaviors presented are somewhat new. Social media is ideal for this type of reinforcement communication. It should echo the main messages delivered by other methods.

Signage, Bulletins, and Letterhead – Almost everything should reinforce the main content of your clear path communication. The unity and consistency of communication can have a powerful effect in helping people quickly and easily orient themselves to the change before them.

Ongoing Listening – Do not expect to perfectly tune your communication with the first message. As you continue to listen to both insiders and outsiders, you will continue to discover gaps in your communication. You must be careful to recognize the difference between resistance and confusion. Some people will indeed resist the changes you are making. Others will fail to engage simply because they do not yet understand what they are being invited to do. Only careful listening and ongoing conversation can discern the difference. If you commit to courageously listening to those who genuinely do not understand, you will be able to fill in the gaps of your communication about your clear path.

WARNING: *Be careful NOT to listen too closely to critiques from those who are disinterested in understanding or are simply resistant to change.* They will discourage and distract you. They may be loud, but they will likely represent a very small portion of the population.

A pastor friend shared with me that when coming into a new parish, he begins by determining the most important needs for the faith journey of his parishioners. Part of that effort is to identify the disposition of various groups of current parishioners. In many cases he says there are those who refuse to try new ideas or ways of doing things. He calls them "the self-appointed, self-important old guard." He says they say things like: "But that's the way we've always done it." This kind of resistance can be tough for pastors, who wonder if people will leave if they do not get their way. Pastors feel a sacred duty to keep the flock together and are afraid to lose any sheep.

Leading a parish community through change is extremely challenging. It requires careful discernment. It requires patient and repeated communication to help people confront their fears surrounding the changes. It also requires tremendous courage as pastors confront their own fears about disappointing people and losing parishioners along the way. A good communication plan is essential, but it will not be enough. Your communication efforts must be covered in prayer.

Communication Step 3: Develop an Intercessory Prayer Team

As you begin to go public with your efforts to build a clear path, you will need a prayer team dedicated to interceding for your efforts. You need the support of prayer warriors who are dedicated to interceding for the development of your clear path at every phase. You will likely feel the need more acutely in the communication phase. The external resistance experienced as you go public will make the need for a team of intercessors clear. The communication phase is the time to employ this team's help if you have not done so already.

Even when negative feedback is the result of a sincere lack of understanding, it is hard to hear. The courage, humility, and perseverance that the communication phase requires will convince you of the need for a team of prayer warriors dedicated to providing supernatural help when building your clear path.

A word for pastors: The communication phase is where the thought of losing parishioners can weigh heavily on pastors. It is true – not everyone will embrace what you are building no matter how well you communicate. The enemy will try to exaggerate the thought of losing parishioners to keep you from making progress. Ironically, this strategy of the enemy is often effective precisely because you care so much about each and every soul.

Lean into prayer and diligent efforts to communicate well. There is no denying that you may lose some parishioners who just cannot understand or accept what you are trying to communicate. Remember that many also went unreached before you set out on this journey to build a clear path. Your conscience is clear when you have done all you can to communicate clearly and effectively.

Communication Step 4: Develop a Clear Path Mantra

The terminology used to describe the steps of a clear path in this book, such as conversion moments and faith formation, etc., are not difficult to understand, but they can be a mouthful. They are a description of the type of ministry you will need at each step. You will need to further simplify the language of your steps to be clear and memorable for parishioners and non-members. The goal is to develop a simple mantra to quickly communicate what is happening in the ministries of your clear path. In Part III's case study, St. Mary's team used "Connect, Know, Grow, and Go." The mantra you choose should communicate your vision for fostering growth and maturity along the sequential steps of your clear path.

At some point, the specific ministries and programs that make up your clear path will need to be intentionally connected to your mantra. For example, people will need to understand that the *Softball Team* helps them "connect" to the parish. *Awakening Retreat* is how they come to "know" Jesus. They "grow" in *Grow Groups*. Evangelization formation ministries, such as *Upper Rooms* training nights, equip them to "go." This will not happen all at once. Be patient. You are dramatically altering people's expectations for what it means to be a good parishioner and how your parish will serve them.

In many ways, your verbal mantra is shorthand for the thresholds of conversion and discipleship or how growth happens in your parish in a general way. The mantra's associated visual icon or image in the next section provides another point of connection to help people recognize exactly how your community will help them grow and mature.

Communication Step 5: Develop a Clear Path Image

In addition to a verbal mantra, a parish's clear path of discipleship also needs a visual representation for parishioners and those who are not yet part of the faith community. Similar to the way public transportation at airports and subways utilize simple language and visual icons to help people connect the dots, a clear path of discipleship also benefits from the use of symbols. Employing the services of a professional graphic designer is not strictly necessary, but it might be helpful. The goal is clarity and simplicity so parishioners can easily self-diagnose their next step and can easily help others do the same.

This is where it all comes together. A good visual image will connect your verbal mantra to the specific ministries and programs that make up your clear path. This connection can happen in several ways. First, an overall image like St. Mary's "Highway to Heaven" provides the mental connection people need to act.

In like manner, the individual symbols for a ministry should always be present in any promotion of an event specific to that ministry. For example, a seasonal faith formation option on the Eucharist would always be accompanied by the *Grow Group* name and image. It might have a tag line like, "Growing in our love of Jesus in the Eucharist."

Communication Pro Tip #1: Personalize Your Target Audience

It can be extremely helpful to make use of what communications professionals call a persona. A persona is simply a made-up character who represents the target audience of your communication. Similar to the task of personalizing your mission field in the discernment phase, communication can be greatly aided by personalizing your target audience. Consider developing a persona for the following groups:

Active Parishioners – What will veteran members of the parish need to hear about the clear path? What will alleviate their fears and inspire their hope?

Inactive Parishioners – What will inactive members of the parish need to hear?

Non-members – What will non-members need to hear so they engage with the invitations they receive?

Spend some time developing a persona for each of these three types of audiences. Think about their age and faith journey. Think about how they will hear the terminology you use. Think about their hopes and fears about sharing their faith with friends, family, neighbors, and co-workers. Spend time in conversation with individuals who embody some of the characteristics of these groups. The time you spend personalizing the various target audiences will directly impact your communication phase's ultimate success.

Communication Pro Tip #2: Use an Orientation Class

Consider utilizing a new members' orientation class to ensure communication about your clear path to new members. After the initial flurry of communication, it could be easy to let communication about your clear path slide off your radar. An orientation class is a great way to communicate your clear path to new members. It is also a wonderful way to engage those members in their next step. For some, that may mean signing up for the conversion retreat. For others, it may mean connecting with a small group. A new members' orientation should clearly communicate how your parish makes and matures disciples. The invitation for a new member's next step should be offered during the gathering.

Communication Pro Tip #3: Don't Stop Until They Finish Your Sentences

A good rule of thumb is to communicate and repeat your message until people begin to finish your sentences. While you always want consistency in messaging, I encourage you to be creative in the methods and expressions of your clear path. Just remember, the real test of communication is when the receivers become communicators themselves. You want people to internalize the message and repeat it as their own. When people start finishing your sentences with some playful mockery, you know you are close to having successfully delivered the message. Smile, and say it one more time.

The communication phase of building a clear path of discipleship can span anywhere from three to six months depending on parish culture, size, and effectiveness of the communication team. However, communication never really ends, and personal invitation persists for life. It is essential to have an intentional, well-planned public communication phase as you build a clear path for making disciples in your parish.

One significant benchmark is if key leaders and staff can quickly and consistently answer the question, "How do we make and mature disciples?" The mantra and the specific ministries of your clear path must be clear to your leaders. They will have the responsibility to communicate it to others. Keep working on it until they know your clear path inside and out.

Communication Pro Tip #4: Honor All Contributions

Ongoing communication should honor all contributions to the clear path, especially those that might seem small or mundane. Every parish activity should be aligned with your clear path. That means every parish activity, in some way, contributes to making disciples and changing lives. A clear path can unite and elevate even the humblest parish activity.

There is a well-known story of President John F. Kennedy's tour of NASA after he committed to join the space race and land a man on the moon. Although the story itself may be an urban legend, the lesson is powerful. On the tour, the president met with engineers, astronauts, and countless others engaged in the epic quest. In passing, the president spoke with one of NASA's janitors. "What do you do here?" asked the president. Without missing a beat, the janitor said, "Mr. President, I'm helping put a man on the moon."

In like manner, everything that happens at our parishes can contribute to the ultimate goal of the salvation of souls. Honor all contributions to the clear path. This great mission to make disciples unifies the parish and gives all parishioners dignity.

Communication Pro Tip #5: Reduce Mass Announcements

I estimate that 90% of Catholics are getting 90% of their exposure to the Church at Mass. Please wisely use this precious opportunity to help connect people to their next steps on your clear path. While not every ministry should be featured in the announcements, the ministries of the clear path must be.

Even if you have other electronic forms of communication, bulletins and Mass announcements are still a primary opportunity to highlight the most important things happening within the parish. These should include the next steps available for growth. Ideally, evangelization and formation will have preceded the Mass, but that is not always a safe assumption for everyone present. Do not hesitate to promote opportunities for people to connect in relational outreach and to attend conversion moments. At the very least, promotion of these opportunities reminds the missionary disciples there is a next step available for them to invite friends and family.

In a similar fashion, Mass announcements are a key opportunity to invite growing disciples to take their next step toward full maturity in Christ. Faith formation and evangelization formation opportunities help take disciples deeper. This makes their experience of the Mass even more meaningful. We are sent out at the end of every Mass. Why not encourage people to take a step that will help them go out more fruitfully? Well-designed announcements can help the weekly Sunday worship bear fruit as people are encouraged to take their next steps to grow and mature.

A Final CAUTION: Longer Than You Think

I would be remiss if I did not offer one more warning about how the communication phase will unfold. *Leaders should always plan for communication to take longer than they expect.* Advertisers know that people need to hear something close to a dozen times before it really registers. The newer the concepts, the more repetition it requires. Leaders typically tire of their message before people have really heard it. While natural, leaders must consciously and intentionally resist the temptation to cease communicating because they are tired of the message.

Despite the relative simplicity of the concepts of a clear path, they present a deceptively challenging communication project. That is because a clear path represents much more than a series of new programs within parish life. It represents a significant shift in culture as an entire community of faith reorients itself toward making disciples. The shift from simply providing pastoral care for members to a more outward looking mission to friends, family, and neighbors is enormous.

Be patient and persistent. You are not just implementing a few new programs. You are undergoing a major cultural shift – something the Church refers to as pastoral conversion. As the name conversion suggests, it also emphasizes the interior work that goes along with our external efforts to communicate. Old habits die hard, especially when they are tied to beliefs about identity. That is why the Church refers to this type of change as pastoral conversion – it feels like conversion. We are saying "no" to a limited understanding of what the Lord is asking, and we are letting him lead us into a new and exciting mission.

Suggested Communication Timeline:

Weeks 1-2: Identify audience and their felt desires. Articulate the clear path in your own words.

Weeks 3-4: Finalize verbal mantra and visual image for the communication channels.

Weeks 5-7: Deliver a homily series.

Week 8: Hold Parish Town Hall and release promotional video.

Weeks 9-12: Initiate face-to-face invitations for people to take their first step on the clear path.

From Communication to Alignment

The ultimate purpose of the communication phase is to help people find their place in this new parish culture. That is where communication moves into alignment. For some, this will be as leaders of ministries. For most, it will be an invitation to connect and grow along the clear path.

Questions for Reflection

1. What are the three concentric circles of communication?

2. Why is repetition in communication about a clear path so key?

3. What will members of your parish need to know to embrace your clear path?

4. What challenges do you foresee as you communicate your clear path to your parish and the wider community?

5. What communication methods do you currently use? Are there additional methods of communication you should consider?

6. How would you give another parish leader a one-minute explanation about why your parish needs to build a clear path of discipleship?

Chapter 10
Phase 5: Alignment

How do existing ministries connect with our clear path?

The alignment phase is all about unity and clarity. It unites all staff and volunteers around the ministries and processes that form your clear path. It goes beyond establishing a common *why* for building a clear path. It also begins to unite all the ministries and activities of the parish around the *what* and *how* of making disciples in this faith community.

The alignment phase also provides additional clarity in the form of simplicity. No matter how well your communication phase is going, many people will not really understand your clear path until some pausing and pruning of certain ministries and activities occurs for the sake of alignment. The purpose of the alignment phase is to bring people into line around the *what* and *how* of your clear path. It is crucial to continue to speak about *why* building a clear path is necessary as a source of unity, so alignment is experienced as unifying rather than divisive.

The alignment phase can often take from six to 18 months, depending on the number of ministries to be aligned and the availability of key leaders for alignment conversations. The effectiveness of communication, which precedes alignment efforts, can also make a significant difference in the time needed for alignment. An effective communication phase can make the alignment phase a little easier.

Returning to the highway metaphor mentioned earlier, a clear path of discipleship might be served by several frontage roads and side streets. Almost any ministry and program could play a role in serving a clear path of discipleship, provided each program leads somewhere. The challenge lies in discerning which programs and ministries provide a context to fruitfully connect people to the clear path of discipleship and which provide unnecessary distraction and dissipation of energy.

There is no getting around the fact that distraction is one of the main obstacles to people's growth as disciples. As noted earlier, too many choices overwhelm and confuse. Another danger is burning out your best leaders. To meet this challenge, there are several steps to align the various ministries and activities in the parish with the clear path of discipleship. (To see an example of the alignment phase, reference the case study in Part III beginning on page 194.)

Alignment Step 1: Develop Your Alignment Questions

Alignment begins with clarity about the goal. There are several questions that can help provide the necessary clarity.

- How might this ministry assist in one of the steps of the clear path (e.g., conversion moment, faith formation, etc.)?
- How can this ministry collaborate with other ministries to help people grow and mature along our clear path?
- What is the capacity of this ministry to move participants toward their next step?
- If this ministry or activity does not directly contribute to making disciples, is it a distraction or a necessary support structure?

Activities that do not assist growth along the clear path, although good in themselves, would not be advertised or scheduled in parish facilities. They may continue simply as activities that parishioners happen to participate in rather than as parish-sponsored ministries. The bridge club, for example, might be full of parishioners, but it is likely not a parish-sponsored ministry. (See Implementation Pro Tip #3.)

Again, be aware that the fear of losing parishioners presents an obstacle to your alignment efforts. Help ensure gentle and pastoral communication by utilizing questions to draw people into self-awareness. Rather than simply telling parishioners what role their ministry may take, invite them into a conversation by asking open-ended questions like those proposed above.

The greater good offered by a clear path is worth the extra effort to engage ministry leaders in conversation. It is also worth the risk that some might walk away for a time. While it is true that not all ministry leaders will immediately jump on board, engaging them in conversation increases the likelihood that they will come around. Another caution – don't write people off. Some may take a sideline stance while the path grows and while they continue to reflect. They may re-engage as they begin to see the fruit.

Alignment Step 2: Develop Your Alignment Plan

Leadership team members and other specially selected leaders should join the pastor in personally visiting parish ministries to help them discern how they might fit into the clear path. What begins with a simple introduction to the vision behind a clear path must eventually develop into a practical discernment about how particular ministries and programs fit in support of a clear path of discipleship. Again, the successes or challenges of the communication phase will influence your plan of alignment. In addition to the alignment questions from Alignment Step 1, two concepts will be key to help existing ministries find their place.

First, it will be helpful to return to the thresholds of conversion and discipleship. Most parish ministries have never thought of themselves in light of the thresholds. Awareness of these thresholds can help ministries recognize who they are best equipped to serve. These conversations with ministry leaders have the potential to dramatically increase the effectiveness of ministries as they narrow the focus of who they serve. They may, of their own accord, begin to internally prune activities not helping them serve their members.

As a reminder, the Thresholds Game is a simple activity designed to introduce the thresholds of conversion and discipleship. It is available online in both English and Spanish at clearpathbook.com.

Second, you must begin to introduce the concept that fruitfulness is more about *sending capacity* than *seating capacity*. Most ministries tend to view success based on how many participants are involved. That is understandable, but short-sighted. Very few ministries are a complete ministry reaching individuals at every threshold of conversion and discipleship. Unless that ministry moves people through all the steps of growth to full maturity in Christ, it will need the help of other ministries. These conversations can help ministries begin to assess their fruitfulness based on how many participants moved from their ministry on to the next step of their journey. After all, forward movement is the real test of success of a ministry designed to help individuals through a particular part of their faith journey.

Alignment Step 3: Pausing

At the outset, too many existing ministries and activities will distract and dissipate the energy necessary for highlighting the clear path and for starting any new ministries that support it.

Leaders will need to ask themselves this question: *Which ministries and programs in the parish need to temporarily pause so the clear path can take root?* Asking ministry leaders to pause some of their activities for a year can be challenging. They must understand why. Even then, it is common to face some resistance.

Emphasizing the temporary nature of the pause year might help ease the discomfort. Almost every ministry was forced to pause (or dramatically scale back) for a year or more during the COVID-19 pandemic. Many ministries returned after the pandemic stronger and healthier than before. The opportunity for rest, reflection, and retooling did not harm healthy ministries with a clear role in the life of the parish.

Most ministries feel the need for more leaders and participants. A clear path of discipleship helps raise the tide for all boats. As more people are welcomed into the community through relational outreach, there are more participants for all ministries. As more individuals experience an encounter with the Lord in conversion moments, there are more disciples who desire to serve and grow in the faith formation programs. Evangelization formation equips current ministry leaders and future ministry leaders for service. When it feels like it is always the same people doing everything, evangelization formation can provide greater numbers of individuals who desire to serve and are equipped for mission.

Finally, it is essential that current ministry leaders and members of the parish involved in various ministries and programs have an opportunity to experience the highlighted ministries in the clear path themselves. *You cannot assume ministry leaders have had a recent conversion experience or that your explanations will connect the dots. People will need firsthand experience.* Many current ministry leaders and parishioners will be the connectors and ambassadors of the clear path ministries to others. They cannot effectively do so unless they have personally experienced the fruit of these ministries. It is not reasonable for most parish leaders and participants to simply add something else to their already full calendars. Making space for current members of the parish to experience the highlighted ministries of the clear path of discipleship often requires them to pause the ways they are currently serving and participating in some ministries.

It might be helpful to acknowledge a difficult reality at this point. Asking people already serving in ministry to experience evangelization training by taking a "ministry gifts assessment" is not going to offend anyone. Almost everyone appreciates the chance to learn about their gifts. It is also not a big deal to offer ongoing faith formation for leaders. After all, nobody knows everything about our faith. But what about inviting veteran leaders into a conversion moment ministry? Does that invitation imply they are not really a disciple?

No. Even faithful disciples need a renewed encounter with the Lord. Just read the story of the disciples on the road to Emmaus (Lk. 24:13-35). They knew and loved Jesus. They had even heard about the resurrection, but they were still confused and discouraged. They needed a renewed encounter with the Lord.

We must recognize that not everyone leading parish ministries is serving from an encounter with Jesus. We must admit that much of what we dismiss as a personality quirk is actually someone trying to serve the Lord through their own strength. Some of the most dedicated and loyal parish leaders are serving out of a sense of duty and obligation and not as an overflow from an encounter with the Lord. For many, it has been quite some time since they had an encounter with the Lord. Some may not be able to think of a recent encounter or conversion moment in their lives. Some may not have really decided to fully give themselves to the Lord. That is not the way it is supposed to be. Our service is supposed to be an overflow of the love we experience in our frequent encounters with the Lord.

If you wonder if this might be the case for some leaders in your parish, you are not alone. We live in strange times when the labels which once carried meaning may not say much about an individual's personal relationship with the Lord. If this is your experience, there is no shame in admitting you need a renewed encounter with Jesus. Remember, the faithful disciples on the road to Emmaus. Jesus comes to them, walks with them, gently corrects their confusion, and invites them to a renewed trust. Using the scriptures and revealing himself in the breaking of the bread, he reignites their hearts. They are changed by the encounter, and they run back to the community, full of joy and ready to share the Good News. Wouldn't it be great if your veteran ministry leaders could find that kind of joy and zeal? Pausing some ministries and inviting veteran leaders to experience steps on your parish's clear path might be just what they most need.

The decision to pause a few ministries as you establish your clear path can be extremely hard. It is, however, necessary and worth the effort. Pausing may be one of the most important things you do, not only to establish a clear path, but to renew leaders currently serving.

Alignment Step 4: Pruning

The most challenging step for alignment is the intentional pruning of some ministries and programs. Keep in mind, a good ministry bearing some fruit can interfere with another ministry becoming excellent and bearing great fruit. Our time, energy, and finances are all finite. A wise and well-discerned decision to prune specific ministries will likely be required at some point when building a clear path of discipleship.

This is challenging for many reasons. First, it can seem as though we are telling the leaders and participants of those programs they do not matter. This could not be further from the truth. They do matter. Their time, energy, and participation are just needed elsewhere. The message should be that underlying needs and desires currently met by that ministry can be better met elsewhere. This message needs to be delivered with appreciation for the people associated with it. Sometimes that need will be met by an alternative ministry within the parish. If appropriate, invitations should be offered. Sometimes these needs are best met outside the parish.

The second reason pruning can be difficult is that we can often only see the loss. All we see is something good going away, and we cannot yet see the good that will come from redirecting energy to new initiatives. Think about pruning in the context of gardening. Wise gardeners know rose bushes must be aggressively pruned and trimmed at the end of the growing season. Failing to do so dramatically reduces the next season's blooms. At the time of pruning, however, the pruning does not look helpful. In fact, a freshly pruned rose bush looks small, dead, and lifeless. It is only in the spring that the wisdom of pruning is verified.

Perhaps one more pruning example is helpful. In John 15, Jesus describes our heavenly Father as a vinedresser. By carefully reading, you will notice God prunes not just dead and lifeless branches but also those that are already bearing fruit. He wants all the energy of the vine to go into a few branches so that they may bear more fruit.

Practically, this means we must be willing to prune and pause programs still positively impacting the lives of participants. It is not enough to prune only those programs no longer bearing fruit. We must wisely prune programs bearing fruit so those remaining will bear more fruit and fruit that will last (Jn. 15:16).

Alignment Step 5: Common Goal Setting

One especially powerful way to establish and maintain alignment is by uniting ministry leaders around a common method of setting goals. The type of goal setting system you choose need not be elaborate or complicated. Simple is best. The only requirements are that the common mission and method of making disciples provide an umbrella for the goals of each staff member, volunteer, or ministry. The process of setting goals aligned to the overarching parish plan for making disciples goes a long way in helping ministries self-align. Additionally, reading goals set by various ministries provides the pastor a pro-active opportunity to recognize and address any misalignment at the start of the goal setting period. Appendices VI and VII help identify clear objectives and provide a simple framework for goal setting.

An additional benefit to common goal setting is that it provides a means for redefining success. In the church world, how we measure success tends to be limited to counting attendees. At one level, this is understandable because what we really seek to produce is hard to measure. Growth and maturity in disciples are not as easy to count as the number of people who attend a retreat, program, or event. Church metrics tend to focus on actions we do rather than outcomes. A common goal setting system allows you to direct attention to actions that tend to produce the desired outcomes.

Most ministries measure their fruitfulness by their seating capacity. *Start to measure fruitfulness by sending capacity.* Begin to ask non-clear path ministries to track how many participants moved from their ministry to the appropriate next step on the clear path. Ask clear path ministries to measure how many people they assisted to move on to the next step on the clear path. Doing this will reinforce the connection between ministries and the purpose of a clear path to foster movement toward making and maturing disciples.

Alignment Pro Tip #1: Expect to Prune in Stages

There is a great pastoral tension in fostering alignment along your clear path. On the one hand, there is a real urgency to build a clear path, make disciples, and change lives for the gospel. On the other hand, the current members of the community are part of the Body of Christ. Alignment is not a corporate restructuring where the loss of members is inconsequential. A commitment to prayer, courageous communication, and deep formation of current members is the route through this narrow valley.

As such, you should expect to prune ministries in stages. You may struggle to recognize ministries that do not fit your clear path. What initially seemed like a helpful connection may ultimately prove to be a distraction in need of pruning. You may unintentionally let fear keep you from having difficult conversations. You might let pushbacks weaken your commitment to simplicity and clarity. Do your best to stay committed to simplicity and clarity. When you see clearly that a particular ministry or leader is not aligned, begin the alignment conversation again.

Alignment Pro Tip #2: Beware of All-Stars

In the world of sports, there is a temptation to think winning is just about talent acquisition. If somehow you could simply assemble a team of all-stars, then winning would be easy. Great coaches know that unity is far more important than having a team of all-stars. A team of average staff or volunteers that are united behind the *why*, *what*, and *how* of making disciples will be more effective than a team of all-stars who are not quite aligned.

This has certainly been true in my own experience of building teams. I appreciate talent and competence, but those gifts can disappoint if more important qualities are not present. Look for a shared passion around your God-given vision. This vision is the foundation for your team's unity, and it must inspire those who are going to be part of your team. You will also need to look for humility, demonstrated by someone with a humble heart willing to embrace the team's plan. When you find teammates who buy into the vision and plan for making disciples, almost anything is possible.

Uniformity, Diversity, and Real Unity

There is a temptation to underestimate the depth of real unity required for making disciples. Sometimes we imagine unity to be uniformity, but we should reject uniformity as impractical and unhelpful. Real unity is much deeper than uniformity. Far from simply having everyone look and act in the same way, real unity is highlighted most dramatically in the context of diversity. In fact, significant diversity exists in the ministry gifts needed for a successful clear path. To function effectively, however, this diversity requires a corresponding unity of purpose.

Saint Paul describes this unity and diversity among a believing community as the body of Christ (1 Cor. 12:14ff). He says the body has many parts, and they all have a specific function. No one part can say to another, "I do not need you." If we carry the analogy into the task of a parish to make disciples, you can imagine the problem if the hands and feet are not working together in unity. Not only must there be a diversity of parts, but each part must also work together in a coordinated fashion. Have you ever tried to walk when one foot has fallen asleep? You are not going to get very far if your feet, your legs, or your whole body are not aligned and working together.

Questions for Reflection

1. Why is pausing often necessary for the development of a clear path of discipleship?

2. What fears or hesitations do you have about pausing or pruning ministries at your parish?

3. What additional benefits do you see resulting from a pause year for your parish?

4. What is the relationship between a multiplicity of programs and mediocrity?

5. Have you ever had to make a difficult decision to prune a good activity out of your life for a better activity or outcome? Share your experience.

6. What method of goal setting do you use personally? What does your team use?

7. What is the danger of trying to build a team of independent all-stars?

Chapter 11
Phase 6: Expansion

What is the next step to build or expand?

The expansion phase is all about building a missing step on the clear path or expanding an existing step to make it more fruitful. Now that you have established some momentum by building one or more steps of your clear path, you can begin to discern construction on the next step. Revisit your blueprint and see if any adjustments are necessary. The phases of discernment, implementation, communication, and alignment may need to be repeated for each new decision to build or expand your clear path.

As you begin to think about building the next step, keep in mind that the next action can often take the form of expanding some existing ministry or program within the parish. That existing ministry may be very small and highly relational. In fact, it might not be recognized as a ministry or program at all. It may be how people are growing and moving naturally.

The next action can also be building a ministry new to your parish. Before you start from scratch, look around. It is likely that what you desire is already happening in another parish or ministry. More than likely, it can be adapted to your unique circumstances.

The challenging part of the expansion phase is filling the gaps and expanding current ministries on the clear path without losing simplicity and clarity. (To see an example of the expansion phase, reference the case study in Part III beginning on page 208.)

Expansion Step 1: Assess the Gaps

The first step in expansion is to assess where your clear path has gaps. These can be identified by revisiting the gaps identified in your initial assessment phase and planned out in your discernment blueprint. It might also mean recognizing where a current ministry on your clear path is not quite producing the desired effect. There are typically three types of gaps: capacity, fruitfulness, and imagination.

A common example of the capacity gap is in the step of faith formation. Once a conversion moment ministry is up and running, it produces people who want faith formation. A conversion moment retreat, for example, might lead 20 or more retreat participants to faith formation after the retreat. However, the current faith formation may not have the capacity to handle all those now interested in growing as disciples.

That is a great problem to have. The need to expand the current faith formation option would then be identified as the next step in your clear path. You might need to train more small group leaders. You might need to purchase additional materials or licenses for online content.

You may also find a gap in the fruitfulness of an existing step in your clear path. This often shows up in evangelization formation. While evangelization formation may begin with a handful of training modules on how to share your faith, over time, it is common for leaders to desire more formation. The further missionary disciples move into the mission field, the more they will be able to tell you what they need to be effective and fruitful.

An imagination gap often happens in the relational outreach step. Thankfully, a successful relational outreach effort shows people how ordinary activities outside of the parish can provide a context for developing trusting relationships with non-members. An example is the men's softball team from the case study in Part III. As more leaders at St. Mary's are equipped for evangelization, their imaginations will grow, sparking their desire to connect with individuals not reached by the softball team.

Over time, the options for relational outreach where people can connect may increase. That is fine if they connect into the main clear path at some point. The most likely point of connection will be the conversion moment and faith formation. So too, the options for evangelization formation may increase as more diverse individuals discover their personal mission and calling. The result is a funnel of sorts resembling an hourglass, which begins in the wider community, converges around the conversion moment, faith formation, and the Mass, and then goes back out into the community.

If this seems overwhelming, please note several things. It is the Holy Spirit who coordinates and generates these increasing options as he calls individuals and endows them with gifts for that mission. The parish and ministry leaders have a role, but it is likely not a controlling coordination of all the types of outreach and formation. Controlling coordination is not needed because a clear path matures disciples. Mature disciples are self-starters and do not need parish money, facilities, or a pastor's presence to turn their hobby into a relational outreach.

This is not to say that the pastor and parish leaders will have no responsibility for the expansion of outreach and evangelization formation. It is just that this responsibility may not be as heavy as you might imagine. It may take the form of occasional mentoring and special emphasis within the existing clear path ministries. An example is a seasonal emphasis on outreach to separated and divorced individuals. One of the conversion moment retreats might offer special accommodation for those who have experienced divorce. The small groups that follow might have materials designed for that need. In that way, the path stays simple while still meeting a variety of needs.

Expansion Step 2: Fill Gaps Where the Holy Spirit Is Already at Work

When I was in college, my school built a new student activity center. It was beautiful and right in the heart of campus. The entire area had been fenced off for the year. As the building was coming to completion, the last phase of construction was to add landscaping and sidewalks. The fencing came down, but weather delayed the completion of the additional sidewalks for a few weeks. When the new sidewalks were finally poured, I noticed something funny. People were not walking on these new sidewalks but along the paths they had trod during the delay.

When it comes to building a clear path of discipleship, we want to avoid paving our own sidewalks when the Holy Spirit is developing other pathways. If the Spirit already seems to be working through individuals, a particular ministry, or methodology, start there. Expanding an existing ministry is far better than creating something new which may or may not be where the Spirit is moving and where people will follow.

Expansion Step 3: Build Frontage Roads

Frontage roads are the routes which run parallel to the main highway. They allow access to stores and businesses not accessible from the main highway. Oftentimes, frontage roads connect with the main highway via on-ramps and exits. Although frontage roads run parallel to the main highway, they are usually lower in elevation and less visible.

By analogy, a parish can have "frontage road" ministries designed for specific demographics that run parallel to the clear path of discipleship. They mirror the clear path in areas with a specific demographic target, (e.g., religious education). Frontage road ministries often intersect the clear path at specific locations, such as a conversion moment or evangelization formation. They are not the main clear path of discipleship, but they have the same features and provide the same benefits. They are just designed for specific age groups or demographics. For example, the programs and ministries that make up the youth ministry program are not as visible to the parish at large, but they provide unity, particularly when they intersect with the highlighted ministries of the parish's clear path.

Aligning ministries for different age groups to your clear path is a huge gift for families. So much in today's world separates family members from one another. That is not the desire of the Church. In fact, if your parish can become a place that helps parents and kids connect with each other, you will quickly earn the loyalty of both groups. The key is to make sure that the path for making disciples is aligned for all age groups and that they occasionally intersect. If you are a parent, you know the path for adults and the path for your kids, and vice versa. Each family member can grow through the same process. When a dad is ready to move into a small group, there is also one available for his daughter.

Expansion Pro Tip #1: Create Complete Ministries

A terrific way to align a specific ministry to your clear path might be as a "complete" ministry. Some ministries, particularly those focused on a specific demographic, have an event or a moment in the ministry which corresponds to each step in the clear path. In this sense, they are what I call a complete ministry. They provide for growth through every threshold and step of the clear path. Youth ministry is a common example. By necessity, youth ministries know how new members connect and where they will likely experience conversion. Leaders have a plan for forming young people as disciples. Sometimes they even have a plan for sending them out.

It is common, however, for ministries to have a solid plan for only three of the four steps of a clear path. The gap of the fourth might simply be an oversight or the need for assistance in creating it. In either case, it can be helpful to discern if there is an opportunity to partner with another ministry for the missing step or if it should be developed within the ministry itself.

As a general rule, collaboration with other ministries gets easier the more individuals mature in their faith journey. Individuals at the beginning thresholds of conversion often need help identifying the people they should connect with next. As people mature and grow along the thresholds of discipleship, there is a beautiful increase in unity across age groups and other demographics. The particulars that once defined us give way to a deeper unity as missionary disciples of Jesus Christ. As a result, people are more open to common formation with those who differ from them in age and backgrounds as they grow and mature as disciples.

Expansion Pro Tip #2: Provide Options Instead

There will inevitably be a moment when a legitimate unmet need surfaces in your community. What will you do? The typical response, and the overwhelming temptation, will be to try to address this need with new programming, special events, or another step on the path. Fight this temptation toward complexity. Instead, provide simple options within existing steps.

Take, for example, the needs of divorced and separated individuals. Many of their unique needs could be met by utilizing existing steps on the clear path. Part of evangelization formation could equip leaders for sensitive conversations with those who are divorced and separated. Those same leaders could facilitate small groups during the main conversion retreat. In like manner, materials designed for those dealing with divorce or separation could provide faith formation during ongoing small groups.

Another example of a special need is financial stewardship. An outreach could be designed specifically for those struggling financially and vulnerable to predatory lenders. Once relationships have been established and immediate needs have been met, outreach could bridge the conversion moment. That conversion moment could be followed with particular small group materials, such as a financial Bible study, for the faith formation step. Finally, leaders could be equipped even more fully to live as stewards and share what they have received with the parish and the larger community.

Expansion Pro Tip #3: Make Special Events Lead Somewhere

All special events must end with a clear "now what?" moment. They must point people directly to a next step on the clear path. Special events make us feel good. They are an easy way to say we care about a cause or need. They can be fun and might bring people together. They can also be a trap. They take time and energy to plan, as well as to staff and find volunteers. They take time and energy for participants to attend. They require time and energy in an already noisy promotional landscape.

Remember the Bradshaw research I cited in Chapter 4 on clarity?[26] There is an inverse relationship between the number of parish-sponsored ministries and special events and its growth. Less is actually more. Special events are not inherently bad, but when they do not connect to your clear path, they can easily become distractions. They must lead somewhere, or they should not exist.

Discerned Expansion

By now you can see that one of the keys to the expansion phase is discernment. The needs presented by a community of believers and a mission field are infinite. Time and energy are not. Not every need represents a call. Not every call requires a programmed or ministry response.

The Lord will guide you through each phase of expansion if you allow him. In some ways this phase never ends. It is a joyful part of the adventure when your parish has begun to send laborers into almost every need within the wider community. Some will become a ministry supported by the entire parish, but most will not. This is the beauty of a clear path – you are preparing laborers for a mission which extends beyond your

---

[26] Travis H. Bradshaw, *Evangelistic Churches: Geographic, Demographic, and Marketing Variables That Facilitate Their Growth*, Ph.D., diss., University of Florida, 2000.

own. That is what it truly means to be a missional community – you are sending formed missionaries out from your parish to the ends of the earth.

May the Lord bless your clear path with many fruitful missionary disciples.

Questions for Reflection

1. What pitfalls must parish leaders be careful to avoid when expanding their clear path of discipleship?
2. What is a "frontage road" for your clear path?
3. How can your parish avoid the trap of complicating your clear path?
4. What is a complete ministry? How might they uniquely contribute to making disciples in your parish?
5. Have you ever personally experienced the power of the Holy Spirit for evangelization?
6. What can you do to ensure your special events lead somewhere?

Part III

A Clear Path Case Study
St. Mary's "Highway to Heaven"

Building St. Mary's "Highway to Heaven"

The story of St. Mary's journey to building a clear path is a fictional case study. The characters and stories are a combination of dozens of real people and real stories. Any resemblance to specific individuals is coincidental.

Father Dave's homily series, "A Highway to Heaven," ended with these words: "Our parish exists to make disciples. That means we are going to help everyone find their next step here at St. Mary's. From those who have no background in faith, to those of you who sing in the choir…the Lord has a next step for you. The Lord wants everyone with him in heaven, so we are building a path to help you **connect, know, grow,** and **go** with Jesus."

To Father Dave's surprise and embarrassment, people clapped. Their reaction was not so much due to Father Dave being a great orator, but he had connected with their hearts. The congregation wanted, even craved, the vision he had shared both for themselves and those they knew who were far away from the Lord.

Behind the scenes, Father Dave and his leadership team worked for more than a year to get to this point. This is their story.

Father Dave's Conversion

This multi-year journey to build a clear path began when Father Dave attended a clergy conference. The presenter challenged the priests of the diocese to start thinking beyond simply keeping the people of their parish faithful. "Part of being a good pastor means helping people mature and become *fruitful*," he said. It helped that the presenter was funny because the material was surprisingly challenging. The priests had all heard the term "missionary disciple" from the writings of Pope Francis, but as the presenter began to draw out some of the logical consequences, things got a little uncomfortable, at least for Father Dave. In retrospect, Father Dave referred to that clergy conference as a type of conversion – a conversion for how he would pastor his flock.

The one-liner that really got him was an old joke that Father Dave himself had often shared with kids in religious education on his classroom visits: "You should always aim for heaven to be a saint. If you only aim for purgatory and you miss," Father Dave would pause, smile, and then one by one the kids would start to smile. They got the point. The clergy conference presenter did the same thing.

He said it this way, "It seems to me that one of the main purposes of our parish communities is to make missionary disciples who can evangelize their family, friends, neighbors, and co-workers. For years we have been settling for a superficial version of discipleship. We haven't been calling our people to prayer and mission. It's like the old joke about aiming for purgatory. If we only aim for faithful disciples and we miss…well, maybe that's why they've stopped coming." Father Dave did not smile, but he did get the point.

The parish needed to make mature missionary disciples. Mature missionary disciples would not only remain in the faith themselves, but they would bring others. As he continued to wrestle with the ideas presented, Father Dave's own prayer and reading began to reinforce what he had heard. Before long, he saw the call to make and mature missionary disciples everywhere.

After a few months, Father Dave decided to share what he had heard at the clergy conference with his parish leadership team. To his surprise, his team quickly grasped the ideas and shared his growing conviction that St. Mary's needed to change. They even helped Father Dave see the necessary changes were not so much a sign that they had failed as leaders, but a product of changing times.

Tom, who owned several local auto body shops, shared a similar phenomenon from firsthand experience. "My grandfather started our first shop, and my dad expanded the business in the '90s. What they did was amazing, but if I tried to run the business the way they did, we would be out of business. My commitment to their legacy required me to make the necessary changes. The principles are the same, customer first and such, but the way we do business today is very different than when Grandpa started."

This was a very freeing insight. Father Dave had started as the pastor of St. Mary's with much energy, and he knew he had done some good things. He had, for example, established a prayer class to teach people methods for personal and conversational prayer, such as Lectio Divina. He had even been able to raise up other leaders who helped teach the class. Teaching prayer was a huge priority for Father Dave coming into St. Mary's. He was absolutely convinced everyone was called to holiness. He also knew personal conversational prayer was essential to holiness. He had wanted to make his parish a school of prayer, and in many ways, he was doing so.

In recent months, however, he frequently found himself at a loss for how to renew his parish. He had let busyness and discouragement creep in and steal his energy. He was stuck. He blamed himself because he did not know what to do next. As pastor, he felt he should have all the answers.

The solution emerged as he shared his new conviction to make mature missionary disciples. His parish leadership team began to ask more questions about the clergy conference. Father Dave shared his notes on the process of evangelization. As they discussed the thresholds of conversion and discipleship, it became clear the parish was not serving people at key points of this process. The clergy conference presenter introduced the idea that a series of ministries designed for specific thresholds could help parishes make and mature disciples. The team was sure they needed to do this. There was so much already happening at the parish. Where should they start? It was hard to wrap their minds around it all.

Father Dave and the team decided to gather a group of key ministry leaders to look at how the current ministries of the parish helped people grow through the thresholds. They gathered leaders to share what had been on their hearts and to introduce the thresholds of conversion and discipleship. Their first session on the thresholds went so well that the team moved quickly to assessing and mapping the current ministries. They used a simple process. They set up giant headers for the thresholds and placed them on a big wall. They printed index cards for all the ministries. They brought good snacks. Then, it was time to assess how their parish made and matured disciples.

St. Mary's Assessment Phase

The assessment phase is about laying a foundation for change by gathering a small number of key parish leaders to cast a vision and assess how current ministries make and mature disciples. (See Chapter 6 beginning on page 93.)

The ministry mapping night at St. Mary's was triumphant, discouraging, and hopeful all at the same time. It was triumphant because all the leaders who shared Father Dave's vision and hopes were together praying and discussing their mission. By this time, Father Dave had been working for a while to educate and form the various leaders of the parish with a vision for the mission. The Pastoral Council had been reading books together. He had offered mini retreats for leaders of various ministries. Whenever he had the chance, Father Dave talked about the new evangelization and the need for the Church to rediscover her missionary identity. All these efforts paid off as the parish leaders came together.

Even with the growing momentum, however, Father Dave and parish leaders felt a bit of discouragement when the assessment revealed just how little they had in place to make and mature disciples. St. Mary's had many activities, but when they assessed which activities made missionary disciples, there were big gaps. It was also discouraging because many of the leaders struggled to grasp the new concepts. Some moments in the conversation were a little tense as a few people became a bit defensive, thinking their programs were being dismissed or devalued.

The conversation about the pancake breakfast almost spun out of control. Some parish leaders saw its potential for welcoming new people and wanted to place it under the seeking threshold as a "relational outreach." They recognized the breakfast as a fun event where someone outside of parish membership could feel welcome.

Others saw the pancake feed as entirely separate from the clear path. In their mind, the breakfast's purpose was not to draw in new people but to make money for the Men's Club. They acknowledged the breakfast's potential to help people connect, but it was not living up to that potential yet. Father Dave's request for Tom to facilitate the assessment was wise. Tom's steady demeanor kept the conversation about pancakes from derailing the entire mapping exercise.

Overall, however, the night was a hopeful beginning. The team began to realize everything Father Dave had been talking about in theory would need to take shape concretely in their parish's ministries and programs. They wanted to have a plan for making disciples at St. Mary's. They wanted something that would engage their children and their fallen-away friends and neighbors. People wanted to be prepared to share their faith in a way that suited them. Their desire and honest assessment were good reasons for hope.

That night was also the first time the team began to use the phrase, "a clear path of discipleship." When they finished the assessment, the wall categorizing their ministries by thresholds was very full. Honestly, it was a bit of a jumbled mess. Someone remarked that the path for someone trying to grow and mature looked like a maze. Tom immediately quipped they had better "clear the path," and the phrase stuck. It became a rallying cry for Father Dave and the team. "We are building a clear path of discipleship," spoke both to their desire to make disciples and to their frustration about the current clutter in the way of this path.

There was another fruit that came from their ministry mapping night. The Holy Spirit had been working on Paul and Anna. They had moved back into the parish about the same time Father Dave arrived at St. Mary's. Paul and Anna connected with Father immediately. Father invited Paul to be on the leadership team, but Paul still had a sense the Lord had something more in mind for his service at St. Mary's. The ministry mapping night sparked something in Paul that would bear fruit in many lives.

Relational Outreach

Relational outreach is a ministry designed to build relationships of trust with individuals who are non-practicing, fallen away, and even non-believers. Its purpose is to provide a context for mature missionary disciples to build relationships of trust. (See Chapter 3 beginning on page 51.)

Relational Outreach

Paul had grown up in the St. Mary's neighborhood. He moved away for college but returned to the parish to be close to family. While he was at college, Paul had a profound encounter with the Lord. He became deeply involved at the Newman Center, the university's student parish. He briefly thought about serving as a missionary after college but never felt a call to full-time missionary work. Following the first meeting with Father Dave and the team, Paul felt called to reach out to men who were not practicing their faith.

Paul was no theologian, but he recognized most men would find going from non-practicing to regular Sunday Mass attendance too big a step. He had tried connecting with other men after Mass, but few people lingered, and the parking lot emptied quickly. Besides, those were the men already coming. His concern was for men who were not setting foot in the church. He had a recurring idea about starting a men's softball team as a place to connect with men from work, but he kept dismissing it…until the ministry mapping night.

On the way home from the ministry mapping, Paul and Anna had an unusual conversation. "Paul, I think Jesus wants you to get a team together and play softball this summer," Anna said. Paul gave a little snorting laugh.

"I think so too. Do you think Jesus will improve my batting average?" he asked.

"I doubt it," Anna replied with a smile.

Paul and Anna both knew a sports outreach could bring men to the parish because they saw it happen in college. The Newman Center used basketball with great effect. They saw countless men, who at first seemed to have no interest in faith, eventually become outstanding Christians and even missionaries. For many of those men, the journey started with basketball games on the quad between the freshman dorms.

Paul hoped softball could do the same thing, especially for his old friend Bill. Bill had been on Paul's mind the whole time the leadership team at St. Mary's talked about the thresholds. Bill and Paul had been friends in grade school but lost touch in high school and college. They had recently reconnected at work, but Bill seemed to have no interest in his faith. He was not hostile about it. He just seemed to be outside with no way back.

Bill had mostly fond memories of growing up Catholic. Bill was not a great student then. He did well enough, learning what he needed to progress from grade to grade. He still remembered those infamous questions in religion class. Bill's youthful eagerness to participate rarely delivered the right answer. Most of the time, he felt like he had struck out with everybody watching.

That was in stark contrast to Bill's success on the athletic field. Bill was good at sports, especially baseball. He missed sports, but it was not the reason he signed up for Paul's softball team. Bill was not at church to see the softball advertisement, but his wife Lori was there. She brought the flyer home. She encouraged Bill to give it a shot, secretly hoping softball with the guys from church might somehow be an avenue for Bill to rekindle his faith. Unknown to Lori, Bill had heard about the softball team on social media and from the guys at work. Bill had already decided to sign up when Paul invited him at one of the company gatherings.

***

The season went well, not so much on the field, but in the dugout and while grabbing a drink after the games. Paul made a point to connect with Bill. Sunflower seeds did the trick. Before long they were just two guys playing softball, but Bill immediately noticed there was something different about Paul.

Bill was always a little distracted by his performance athletically. Having played in high school and junior college, Bill had unreasonable expectations for his 40-year-old body.

Paul, on the other hand, seemed remarkably free. He was competitive and wanted to win, but he never let a bad call or a mistake ruin his fun.

Bill also noticed Paul seemed genuinely interested in him and his teammates. Paul remembered what they talked about the week before, and he asked questions about Bill's family beyond the superficial "bro talk" Bill had come to expect from most of his other friendships.

St. Mary's Discernment Phase

The discernment phase of building a clear path of discipleship is about developing a blueprint for the future programs that will make up the clear path. (See Chapter 7 beginning on page 106.)

Assessing the ministries went well, so Father Dave and the team had some confidence moving forward in building a clear path. They began the difficult challenge of discerning what their clear path of discipleship should look like. They had some good ministries, but they also had big gaps. They knew not every ministry would be part of their clear path. Real discernment was going to be necessary to develop their clear path.

Father Dave was determined to enter the discernment process as deeply as possible. He had been burned too many times by the work of well-meaning committees that added a long list of to-dos to his plate. He was confident the Lord wanted them to do something new. He was also confident he only had the time to do what the Lord was really asking.

By chance, Father Dave stumbled across a method for discernment while talking to Tim, an old friend from seminary. Tim joined a religious order rather than serving in a diocese. As part of his religious vows, Tim received the name Father Ambrose. Father Dave arranged his vacation so he could stop at the monastery to visit his old friend.

As they talked, Father Dave shared his concerns about the process he was undertaking at St. Mary's to build a clear path of discipleship. It took about an hour, but with the help of his friend's gentle questions, Father Dave finally figured out what was really bothering him.

"Tim, I mean Ambrose, I think what I really want is a simple way to invite my people to discern with me," Father Dave said. "Most of them would get lost in the language we learned in seminary about discernment. They know how to pray, but they are not theologians. I am confident they hear God's voice, but I do not know how to guide them through the process as a group."

"It sounds like you need something that's both familiar and communal," said Father Ambrose with a smile. He proceeded to share the process he used to discern entering the monastery. "I just went to our mother, Mary, in the Rosary, only I did not meditate on the mysteries. I meditated on the questions in my heart. I brought her specific questions and prayed each decade with one of my questions. I listened as I prayed. The familiar repetition of the Rosary helped me quiet my mind so I could hear what the Lord was saying in response to my questions."

Father Dave knew this was the answer to his dilemma. St. Mary's parishioners had a strong devotion to Mary. Father Dave had done his best to deepen and cultivate it right from the start. It seemed fitting to use the familiar prayer of the Rosary to help his leaders join him in discernment about building a clear path. Everyone loved it. They prayed the "Discernment Rosary" with Father Dave on four separate nights and even committed to prepare with a simple fast, like the one observed on Ash Wednesday.

When they were finished, Father Dave and the team had a plan for what their clear path of discipleship would look like. It was a blueprint that would guide their efforts to build a clear path. At least it was a start.

St. Mary's Initial Clear Path Blueprint

As they began to discern, Father Dave and the team quickly realized the Awakening Retreat[27] was going to be their primary conversion moment. The retreat had great momentum and was already producing conversion in the lives of those who attended. It was not technically a parish retreat, but it was working. There was no need to reinvent the wheel.

The assessment phase revealed St. Mary's did not have much in place for relational outreach except softball. The first summer of softball had gone so well, Father and his team decided the St. Mary's team in the city softball league would be their relational outreach. It was working for both the men and their wives. The wives got to know each other on the sidelines, and the kids played on the adjoining playground. Sometimes people would even tailgate. There was a need to find and develop new leaders for this endeavor, but they were confident the softball team would be one of their main efforts for relational outreach.

The conversation on evangelization formation was a little more difficult. Angie, one of the leadership team members, had some valuable experience, but there was not much interest on the part of parishioners yet. In the end, the team realized they were not ready to develop a formal ministry for evangelization formation. They did not know what it would look like, but they felt peaceful and confident the Lord would provide when the time was right. In the meantime, the leadership team would host speakers on evangelization twice a year. They agreed to wait patiently for the Lord to show them the next step for evangelization formation.

The big surprise was their difficulty discerning the faith formation step. Father Dave and his team initially thought this would be the easiest part of the conversation since there were

---

[27] Awakening Retreats are very loosely affiliated retreats often utilized by campus ministries to share the core gospel message and connect retreatants with real friends within the parish.

so many existing programs and ministries categorized in this step. Ultimately, this was the problem. All the existing programs provided solid content, but none of them really seemed to transform lives. The leaders were very dedicated. Ironically, this created an additional challenge. Some of the faith formation leaders were more dedicated to their specific ministry than to the larger parish mission to make disciples.

There was another obstacle to discerning a step for faith formation. Father Dave anticipated resistance to highlighting just one or two ministries. He was committed to making disciples, and he knew things had to change. Unfortunately, his fear of disappointing others and of appearing to show favoritism complicated things. As a result, the team struggled to simplify or create clarity for the faith formation step.

Due to these fears, Father Dave and the team decided to highlight four existing faith formation programs rather than one or two as part of their initial clear path blueprint. While it did not go far enough to provide true clarity, it was a start.

The team did have clarity about wanting faith formation to be different. They implemented a rule that no one could do faith formation without food. Ministry leaders were encouraged "whenever possible" to offer faith formation activities at facilities other than the parish hall. Father Dave would say half-jokingly, "Fluorescent lights and metal chairs keep the faith from sticking." People were encouraged to gather in smaller groups in their homes. Most importantly, every faith formation ministry event had to be marked by substantial time in some form of relational prayer. Taken together, Father Dave's "rules" began to improve the experience of participants in the various faith formation choices.

Conversion Moment

A conversion moment is a ministry designed to foster an encounter with Jesus and a call to conversion. This may be a renewed encounter for a disciple, or it may be an initial conversion for those with no previous connection with the person of Jesus. (See Chapter 3 beginning on page 51.)

Conversion Moment

At St. Mary's, the conversion moment became the Awakening Retreat, a weekend retreat offered by a local ecclesial movement. The format of the retreat was simple. It involved formal talks and personal witnesses where people could share their own stories about their encounters with the Lord. Small group discussions were interspersed for participants to process their thoughts with a few other retreatants and a veteran leader.

Father Dave had experienced the Awakening Retreat years before as a new assistant in another parish. He was sold on the power of the retreat, but he initially had mixed feelings about his role in recruiting. For years, Father Dave included notices about the retreat in the bulletin. He would even offer personal encouragement to some individuals, but he hesitated to publicly endorse the retreat from the pulpit. The Awakening Retreat was not technically a parish program, but that was not Father Dave's concern.

He was afraid that a more public promotion of the retreat would be perceived as favoritism. Father Dave knew how deadly favoritism could be in a family. He knew the retreat changed lives, but his fear of showing favorites kept him from really recruiting with passion. Ultimately, his decision to promote the retreat came in a moment of exasperation.

In a way, you could say the slow sign-ups for the parish festival pushed Father Dave over the edge. It was the ring toss again. Each year it was harder and harder to find volunteers to run the games. As much as he wanted to let the committee chairs run the festival, he had a sinking feeling he would need to get personally involved in recruiting again.

Paul's wife, Anna, was on the festival committee. The committee could feel Father Dave's frustration as weeks passed and signups remained slow. As the time for the festival came closer, Anna made an off-hand comment that would change everything.

"Wouldn't it be great if we put the same energy into recruiting for the Awakening Retreat as we do for the festival's ring toss?" she asked.

That did it. In a mysterious moment of grace, Father Dave saw everything clearly. The messages for growth and involvement at St. Mary's were a jumbled mess. The bulletin boards looked like an overgrown weed patch, and the Mass announcements lasted forever. The bulletin was five pages long in eight-point font. Nobody knew what really mattered. The only indication of true importance came when Father was involved personally, which is why everyone invited him to be involved in everything.

In an instant, Father Dave recognized he was not being true to his own heart. His fear of disappointing people and showing favoritism had kept him from being clear about what he and the Lord most wanted for his people.

The next Sunday Father Dave spoke from the heart. He cut all the announcements except one and told his own story of conversion.

"If you want a taste of what the Lord did in my life, I urge you to come to the Awakening Retreat," he said. "If it is not for you, maybe this invitation is for someone else. Please do not be afraid of rejection. Take the chance and make an invitation. Let's see what the Lord can do."

Paul had committed to praying for Bill as part of the softball team. When he prayed, he often thought he should invite Bill to the retreat. Paul always managed to find a reason to dismiss that thought as crazy. Father Dave's homily was the final push Paul needed.

It was hard to say who was more surprised when Bill agreed to join Paul on the retreat. Bill's wife Lori laughed aloud when Bill first said he was going, but then she realized Bill was serious. Despite his decision to make the invitation, Paul was sure Bill would say no. To tell the truth, Bill was sure Bill would say no. One of the other guys on the softball team had passed out the retreat flyer the week before and made a general invitation to the group. But when Paul made a personal invitation, Bill said yes.

The Awakening Retreat changed Bill's life. Everything worked together – the stories, the talks, and the time in prayer before the Blessed Sacrament. The highlight was Bill's exceptionally long confession. It had been a few years since he had experienced the sacrament. Bill felt sorry for the guy in line behind him. Paul was there with Bill the entire time. Well, he was not with him in the confessional, but he was there during the retreat and in the critical months that followed.

St. Mary's Implementation Phase

The implementation phase is where the clear path begins to come to life. It is where a parish begins to take concrete steps to build or to refine a particular ministry as a step on their clear path of discipleship. (See Chapter 8 beginning on page 116.)

While the Lord was powerfully at work in Bill's life, Father Dave and the parish leadership team were hitting a ceiling regarding their time and capacity.

The Lord had previously used Tom's experience in business to positively impact Father Dave and the team. When they confused the need to change with an indication of failure, Tom's voice had been a gift from God, helping them overcome discouragement. However, as they moved to discuss implementation, Father Dave wondered if Tom had become the voice of the devil.

Tom was relentless, repeatedly saying, "We need to do this, and we need to do it now." Tom was not wrong about the urgency. The eternal salvation of souls was an urgent matter. But it sounded like "we" really meant Father Dave and a handful of people who already felt maxed out. Moreover, Tom's "this" sounded like building the entire clear path all at once. It was too much.

Tom's offer to help was sincere, but it felt disingenuous because everyone knew he really did not have the time to build a new ministry for St. Mary's clear path. The spirit was willing, but the schedule was full.

Full schedules were a problem for everyone. Busyness plagued Father Dave and the entire team from staff to volunteer leaders. They did not have the time nor the bandwidth to build a complete plan for moving forward. From a certain perspective, busyness was also one of the main obstacles keeping parishioners from taking their next step in the journey.

After many long and intense conversations, the team eventually settled on Father Dave's "rules for faith formation" as their first action in building a clear path of discipleship at St. Mary's (offer food, meet off parish grounds, and include time for relational prayer). As the team continued to wrestle with how to move forward, they clearly recognized the importance of capitalizing on the current momentum within the faith formation programs.

This is where Tom began to be helpful again. "We're going to need more than just a few rules for faith formation," he said. "We're going to need to teach people the *why* behind these 'rules.'"

Tom went on to share an example from his personal business. He noticed that a detailed manual for how to run a shop was only part of what made a particular location successful. "Don't get me wrong," Tom said. "We paid good money for a consultant to help us develop that manual. It spells out very clearly the process for how things get done. But I was missing shop managers who understood *why* things had to be done a certain way."

What Tom said made sense to everyone. In the end, the team decided on a combination of approaches to help current faith formation leaders understand the *why* behind Father Dave's rules for faith formation. They felt good about the shared clarity and understanding of the rules. They even had a checklist of the key ideas they needed to communicate to ministry leaders. Unfortunately, the team still lacked a plan and a leader who could bring that plan to life. For Father Dave's vision for faith formation to materialize, they needed more help.

This is where Janice entered the story. Janice had served on the Pastoral Council for almost a decade. Nobody loved St. Mary's more than Janice, and few people did as much in service for the community. Over the last year Father Dave had begun to speak with the Pastoral Council about the dreams growing in his heart and mind. Some of the presentations were formal, but most were just short snippets he gave in the "pastor's comments" section of the monthly Pastoral Council meetings. Slowly but surely, Father Dave had begun to change the purpose and the makeup of the Pastoral Council. As the challenge of guiding St. Mary's into mission led him further into uncharted territory, Father Dave began to seek wise and prayerful counsel.

Janice was both wise and prayerful, but at heart, Janice was a doer. She had been invited to serve on the Pastoral Council when it functioned as a governing body for parish activities and volunteer groups. Not only did they receive reports from the various ministries and programs, but most of the Pastoral Council members were in leadership roles helping to make those activities happen.

Father Dave had a new vision for his Pastoral Council. "I need your help thinking," he said. "There are a lot of people who are generously giving their time and energy to make things happen, but I need you to help me think strategically about the direction of the parish." When Father Dave first began to say these things, it felt like a compliment to Janice. But her frustration built as the team began to spend more time thinking and less time doing.

It came to a head one night at the regular monthly council meeting. Father Dave suggested the Pastoral Council spend a whole Saturday together in prayer and conversation about the new Vatican document on parish renewal. What had been festering in Janice just came out. It surprised her and everyone else.

"Are you kidding?" she said. "We've got so much to do, and all you want to do is get us together to talk and pray?"

The awkward silence that followed brought Janice back to her senses. Janice quickly apologized and said she was happy to come some Saturday next month.

"I do believe in prayer," she added.

"I know you do," Father Dave said with an awkward smile. "Why don't we finish scheduling now, and maybe you and I can talk a little bit more after the meeting?"

The conversation ultimately was a gift for both Father and Janice. The key moment came when Father Dave just said it plainly. "Janice, we call it a Pastoral Council because I need you all to offer me the gift of counsel," he said. "You're great at getting things done, but that's not the purpose of this council anymore."

After a moment, Janice soberly and respectfully replied that she should probably resign from the council. In that same moment Father Dave had an epiphany. He began to smile and almost laugh.

"Janice, I think you're right," he said. "But that doesn't mean I don't need your help." Surprised, Janice just stared at him and blinked.

"Janice, I need your help getting our clear path started. I just realized as we were talking that our dream of building a clear path will never come to fruition without a doer like you. I need you to help me get this done. I trust you, and I know you believe in the vision," he said. "Would you be willing to step off the Pastoral Council and help us bring our clear path to life?"

Janice did not doubt Father Dave's sincerity, but she was still a little shocked. She told him she wanted some time to think about it. That was a Wednesday night. By Thursday morning, he had a long e-mail waiting for him.

The Holy Spirit had been at work on Janice. She loved getting things done and missed serving in that way. She had spent a good couple of hours in the adoration chapel processing the council meeting and reviewing her journal for the last few months. By the time she left the chapel, Janice was almost running to the car to get back home and compose her email.

Far from being one of those long, unpleasant emails pastors sometimes receive, Janice's e-mail made Father Dave weep for joy. She wasted no time with sentimentality and had already outlined a plan for educating the faith formation leaders on Father Dave's rules. Janice was a project manager, who worked at a regional level for a local bank, and she had a gift for hospitality. She also had some critical experience as a corporate trainer. This was where her professional background and her gifts for service in the kingdom all came together.

It was only a project plan, but Father Dave thought it was beautiful. He reflected on how he had been anxious during the discernment process about who could help build their next step. It was not his strength, and he knew it. Only now did he recognize the need for someone like Janice, and before he could even ask, the Lord had provided. That helped Father Dave understand his tears. He was not weeping about a project plan. He was overwhelmed with gratitude at how the Lord was providing for them in this process.

Janice's plan to gather leaders for formation around Father Dave's rules was fantastic. Although no one recognized it then, her work in establishing this plan eventually became one of the main vehicles for evangelization formation. They called it, Upper Rooms (Acts 1:13ff). The Upper Rooms would replace the guest speaker series on evangelization. The format of the nights would adapt and grow, but true to her reputation, Janice got things off the ground.

Faith Formation

Faith formation is a ministry designed to support disciples as they grow in the knowledge and habits of Christian life. New believers need more than just information. As the Lord continues his work in their lives, they need accompaniment and role models for how to live as a disciple. (See Chapter 3 beginning on page 51.)

God's timing was perfect. The Awakening Retreat that so profoundly impacted Bill happened a few weeks before the start of Janice's first Upper Rooms. Paul and Anna were so grateful for what the Lord was doing in Bill and Lori's lives, but they had not thought much about what might be next. At the first Upper Rooms, Father Dave told a story of his own experience in a small group as he discerned entering the seminary. That story provided the inspiration Paul and Anna needed. They decided to start a small group for Lent and invite Bill and Lori. The group met on Sunday nights in their home with the treats everyone had given up for Lent.

Anna and Lori had become friends during the softball games. The other couples all loosely knew each other. Paul led the group through Lectio Divina, a slow prayerful reading of the scriptures. He used short selections from the next Sunday's gospel. Paul had learned how to pray with the scriptures in college. The experience impacted everyone. Although he was not much of a teacher, Paul led it because it was not really teaching. He started with some fun conversation starters to get people warmed up, and then he read the scripture passage slowly and prayerfully. Paul's main contribution was just modeling his own conversational prayer and walking the group through the repeated readings of Lectio Divina. The Holy Spirit did the real work.

Inevitably, something would stir in someone's mind, and that overflowed into a conversation after the prayer was done. Paul was amazed how often the conversation would move into an area he and Anna had personally wrestled with or learned about a few weeks before the meeting. Sometimes people would stay late and watch a short video clip on a special topic. Other times the conversation concluded with a book recommendation, not just from Paul and Anna, but from other group members.

Bill was soaking everything up. He was full of questions. He felt like everything about church and his relationship with God was new.

Bill's growth as part of the small group with Paul gave Father Dave and the team a breakthrough. Even with Father Dave's rules, all the formal programs of faith formation currently at St. Mary's had a heavy emphasis on information but did little to teach people how to pray. The programs also rarely cultivated a sense of community. These missing pieces were part of the small group that made Bill's experience so transformational. Realizing the power of prayer and community for forming new disciples helped crystalize their desired outcome from faith formation. Reflecting on what the Lord had done in Bill's life helped Father Dave and the team settle on the faith formation step for their clear path. Even more, they began to see the role small groups could play for every step on their clear path.

Father Dave and the leadership team leaned in the direction of creating small groups in every ministry. Eventually they called their small group initiative for faith formation, Grow Groups. The name helped everyone recognize Grow Groups were designed to help people grow. They offered several options for materials to address the wide spectrum of faith formation needs. The small group format provided the community, prayer, and food that solidified the faith formation. There were enough options to fit diverse needs, but the path remained simple and clear.

Gaps in Understanding

Ironically, Janice's success in building the Upper Rooms still did not mean she really understood where Father Dave was trying to lead the parish. It was her sincere confusion that signaled the need for more communication.

One night after a great Upper Rooms, as Father Dave intended to say a quick thank you and goodnight, Janice casually remarked, "You know, I appreciate what you are trying to do for our parish, but I still don't really get what you mean when you say, 'The Church exists to evangelize.' I don't know what that means practically."

Father Dave felt he had been sharing the vision successfully, so Janice's question was a little discouraging. Luckily, it had been a great night, and he could hear the sincerity in her question. He took a big breath and searched for the right words.

"Well, Jesus came to reconcile the world to God. The world is hostile to God. That hostility wrecks our hearts and minds," he said. "Jesus invites us into that reconciliation mission as ambassadors. It begins with us personally being reconciled to God and each other. Ultimately, we extend that reconciliation to our friends, family, neighbors, and co-workers."

"So, this is about us being ambassadors to those we know?" asked Janice, finally looking up from cleaning the table. Father Dave smiled and nodded.

"Yes, that is evangelization and the mission of our parish," he said. "It's just hard because we have forgotten how. Basically, all of us need to learn how to talk to people in our lives about Jesus."

"That is going to take a lot of work," Janice said. "That's just not how most of us were raised in the faith."

"Well, that's why I am so glad I have your help," he said feeling satisfied that it seemed to make sense to her.

"Well, I am happy to help," she said, "but if 'all of us' are going to learn this, don't you think you should tell 'all of us' where we are headed?"

"I can't really argue with that," said Father Dave.

It was time to start communicating more broadly.

St. Mary's Communication Phase

The communication phase is where you go public with broadscale communication of your plans and efforts to build a clear path. (See Chapter 9 beginning on page 125.)

There is no doubt the name, "Highway to Heaven," for Father Dave's homily series on the clear path was a little corny, but the homily series solidified the name of St. Mary's clear path journey. Father Dave preached on the clear path for three weeks during the Easter season. It fit perfectly with the Mass readings from Acts of the Apostles, and he did a fantastic job.

Father Dave was a good preacher. The problem was that preaching was his only plan for sharing their clear path. As the team reviewed the homily series during a regular leadership meeting, Tom mentioned the gap in communications.

"Father, that was awesome. You were clear, passionate, and you connected with people's hearts," Tom said. "I even heard people repeating your phrase on the way out. 'The Lord wants everyone with him in heaven.' I just have one question. What's next?"

Father Dave was elated and deflated at the same time. "What do you mean?" he said. "We're going to finish building it and let the Lord change lives."

Tom explained he thought additional communication was needed. At first, Father Dave was defensive. He initially thought Tom was reopening an old debate about how long the sermon series should be, but Angie spoke up to clarify. Angie said she agreed with Tom. Father had done a fantastic job on the sermon series, but she could tell things were not totally connected yet.

"I've talked to some people," she said. "Although they love what you said, they're wondering how they fit in this clear path thing. This is still new for them. Remember, we've been thinking about this for a long time."

"Actually, I'm pretty concerned about how people are responding," said Dawn. Despite her background as a teacher,

Dawn was the quietest member of the team. "Everybody thinks you're playing favorites, Father," she sighed.

You could have heard a pin drop.

"Everybody?" Tom asked in obvious frustration. Dawn retracted a bit and said there were a handful of veteran faith formation leaders who resented that some ministries seemed to be singled out as special.

The fear of favoritism had kept Father Dave and the team from fully embracing simplicity when they first started to develop their clear path. Now it was causing confusion because there were still too many choices. In an attempt to remedy the situation, the team decided all faith formation opportunities could continue if they followed Father Dave's rules, but only Grow Groups would be highlighted as part of their clear path. Family faith formation for religious education would also be highlighted since it mirrored the clear path for adults and helped engage parents and children together.

After a long and winding discussion, the team made a plan to contact individual leaders who felt frustrated by the decision to highlight fewer ministries.

The next week, the leadership team gathered and recounted their conversations with the faith formation leaders. It was clear there was a communication problem. Almost everyone liked the ideas behind the clear path, but concern over what appeared to be preferential treatment of a few ministries threatened to sabotage unity for building the clear path. The whole team was discouraged, especially Father Dave. It felt as if their whole effort at building a clear path was in jeopardy, until Tom reminded the team how people loved the core idea. "It seems like they just need more information," he said.

Tom suggested the parish hire a consultant to help develop a comprehensive communication plan for their clear path of discipleship. Despite his initial nervousness about how Father Dave would respond, Tom was confident the team needed the help of a professional. He and his wife had discussed the matter, and he offered to pay for the service personally.

"I've worked with this person before in my business," he said. "Father Dave, you are a great communicator, but I think we need help thinking through how to leverage your gifts and communicate in a comprehensive way."

Tom's idea was a relief to Father Dave and the team. They were beginning to recognize that their communication efforts needed to be much broader and longer than they originally imagined. The idea of getting professional help seemed to confirm the importance of the task of building their clear path. They were eager to have a guide because they wanted to get to the destination.

The team decided to work with Diane, the consultant Tom recommended. Diane was not Catholic, but she was a faithful Christian with an evangelical background. She loved Jesus and had experienced her own conversion as part of a faith community committed to evangelization. She had a background in marketing, communications, and project planning. Her friendship with Tom had made her curious about the Catholic Church. After many years of working with Tom as a consultant, she happily agreed to help St. Mary's.

When Diane believed in a project, she gave it her all. The desire to help her friend Tom and her curiosity about the Catholic Church combined to draw her in to the St. Mary's clear path project. She wanted to see the parish succeed. She became a coach, seeing the best in the team, even when they sometimes doubted themselves.

Over several weeks, Diane guided Father Dave and the team through developing a comprehensive communication plan. She introduced the concentric circles of communication to help them recognize how their communication needed to be specific for various parish groups. As she was drawing out the three circles she said, "Your key leaders will need to be **involved** in the building, the whole parish will need to be **informed**...." Before she could finish, Father Dave interrupted.

He appreciated everything Diane was saying, but he could not imagine who was going to be in the outermost circle. When he asked who was in the final circle, Diane gave him a blank stare, and then started to laugh. "That's the larger community," she said. "Your neighborhood and all the non-members that your members' lives touch. They must be **invited**."

Diane's graciousness and charm softened Father Dave's embarrassment. His pastor's heart was so focused on helping his parishioners understand and commit to answering the Lord's call that he had briefly forgotten those on the outside. They were not just trying to get each other to heaven – they had a mission to the whole neighborhood.

Father Dave could hear his own words, "The Lord wants everyone with him in heaven…." He was the pastor of every soul in their parish boundaries, not just the Catholics. He was not just trying to help his people become faithful disciples. He was trying to help his people become fruitful missionary disciples. That was the original inspiration. He had momentarily forgotten it in the whirlwind of building the clear path.

Diane also encouraged Father Dave to deputize the team to join him in face-to-face communication. They spent some time brainstorming the names of key leaders and assigning those leaders to leadership team members with whom they already had strong relationships. They divided existing ministries into groups to visit. Each group of ministries received a personal presentation of the plan and an explanation of their part. Diane helped them develop common talking points, a simple script, and a list of frequently asked questions.

Anna and the Seven Sisters

Paul's wife Anna loved what was happening at St. Mary's. At the start, both Anna and Paul were part of Father Dave's leadership team. After a year or so, Anna decided she needed to be more present for her three children who were still living at home. When she first decided to step back from the team, she thought she would be left out of the process. As things turned out, she played a more vital role than ever through her prayers.

Father Dave especially treasured Anna's prayers. As her pastor, he had counseled her many times that faithfulness to God's will in the moment released grace. A natural routine developed for Anna to receive regular updates from Father Dave and Paul. She would lift them up in prayer during her week, especially when her toddler was being difficult. Sometimes she wondered if his tantrums in the middle of the grocery store were somehow releasing extra grace for Father Dave and the team. Every now and then she offered a text update of her own, "Timmy just cut his sister's hair…and tried to glue it back on… offering this up for you all."

In addition to her gifts for prayer, Anna was also a natural "connector." Anna could talk to anyone, or more accurately she could get anyone to talk to her. Like other young moms in the parish who had made decisions to step back from the workforce while their children were young, she felt the loss of social connections that work had provided. Anna's own needs for connection and her desire to be a part of the parish evangelization efforts came together as she recognized herself as a connector for young moms. Before long, Anna was forming a community of women who supported each other as moms and as growing disciples. They would take turns watching each other's kids so that they could attend retreats and take advantage of other opportunities for growth.

In time, Anna began to draw the other moms deeper into prayer for the St. Mary's team. They called themselves the Seven Sisters.[28] The moms would each take a specific day of the week to pray for Father Dave and the team's intentions. Anna provided low-level coordination of the group by passing along prayer requests. No one outside Father Dave and the

---

[28] The Seven Sisters Apostolate is a wonderful ministry. For more information visit sevensistersapostolate.org.

team knew the role the Seven Sisters were playing, but in many ways, they were the secret power keeping things moving forward even when things appeared to be stuck.

One of these times was the development of evangelization formation for Upper Rooms. The team had hoped Upper Rooms would equip people for their personal mission to evangelize, but something was not working. Janice was exceptionally gifted at getting things done, but her role in Upper Rooms focused only on logistics. Father Dave handled all the content. Upper Rooms were good, but they failed to translate into action for those in attendance. No one quite knew what to do, so they agreed to pray about it. Anna and the Seven Sisters got to work on it as well.

The prayer led to conversations between Janice and the leadership team about the Upper Rooms' purpose. "What do we want people to do after they attend Upper Rooms?" Janice asked.

"I guess we want them to go out," Father said with a little laugh.

"Okay. Rather than just *tell* them to go out, let's give them the skills they need when they go out," said Angie. The conversations brought back all of Janice's corporate training experience. Janice quickly brought Angie into the conversation, and together they made a plan, not simply to inspire, but to equip people with practical skills for sharing their faith. Skills, such as sharing your faith story and starting a spiritual conversation, became the main content. This subtle shift made all the difference.

Evangelization Formation

Evangelization formation is a ministry designed to equip disciples as they are sent out on mission through the power of the Holy Spirit. (See Chapter 3 beginning on page 51.)

In addition to the skills taught at Upper Rooms, St. Mary's evangelization formation used a ministry gifts assessment to help people discover their personal mission. People took the assessment and then met individually with Father Dave or Angie to discuss the results. At first, the team expected everyone to continue to serve in the specific ministry in which they currently were serving. It was a natural mistake. There were so many leadership needs in the parish ministries.

The Lord's work surprised them. As the team accompanied individuals in a spirit of true discernment, they noticed how many people were being called to a personal mission outside the parish. The Lord would call them to serve on the public school board, to evangelize to their neighbors, or to be a witness to their co-workers. In faith, Father Dave and the others stopped trying to artificially direct people toward parish ministries and started letting the Lord call people into their personal mission, regardless of where they landed. It was beautiful to watch the Lord work in the lives of these disciples.

Slowly, the apparent scarcity of help began to disappear. Internal squabbling gave way to a greater sense of unity in making disciples. New and unexpected leaders began to emerge. Some felt called to serve in parish ministries. Others felt called to serve in the greater community. Countless more just began to share their faith with fallen-away, unchurched friends, as well as non-Christian neighbors. Disciples were being equipped for mission. The fruit was undeniable even when it manifested in unexpected ways.

Paul, for example, thought Bill should take over the softball team outreach. It was natural, given Bill's background as an athlete and his outgoing personality. Besides, Paul was getting a little tired. It was a hard conversation when Bill told Paul he did not think the Lord was calling him to serve there.

Bill's decision was the fruit of prayer and solid discernment. Bill was indeed made for outreach, but he was feeling drawn to help a new group of guys at work. He felt softball was just not the right avenue. His co-workers were good men, and many had been raised in Christian homes, but their faith was only skin-deep. After spending months in the couples' Grow Group with Paul and Anna, Bill began to recognize how prayer with scripture could be a moment of encounter.

Bill's call to teach his co-workers to pray surprised him. Bill had always been a little uneasy about discussing faith at work, but now he felt he had something to offer. The freshness of his own conversion gave Bill a passion his co-workers found attractive. His experience in learning to pray with scripture gave him the courage to invite his co-workers to pray together over lunch. Bill did the same thing he had watched Paul do with the couples' group on Sunday evenings. Before long, these men were asking sincere questions.

At this point, Bill's enthusiasm hit a roadblock. Many of Bill's co-workers were not Catholic. Most would have described themselves as Christians, but they were struggling with the "Catholic stuff." Bill was at a loss to answer most of their questions. "I can't explain why. It just makes sense to me," was Bill's typical answer. Not surprisingly, this was not especially satisfying to the guys at work. Bill was getting frustrated, and he was tempted to give up.

The solution came when Paul invited Bill to attend an Upper Rooms night at St. Mary's. Paul could tell Bill needed the support of other missionary disciples trying to share their faith. He also realized he could not give Bill everything necessary to grow in this part of his journey. A wider community was necessary for Bill to continue to grow. The Upper Rooms night also introduced Bill to Angie.

Angie had served as a missionary in Ireland between college and her current job at a local bank. "It's not like you see in the movies," she told Bill. "Ireland is pretty secular now. Dublin is like New York. It just has a different accent."

Angie's missionary training had equipped her to answer both cultural objections to the faith and questions raised by other Christian denominations.

Angie helped Bill learn how to answer questions from the guys at work. She patiently mentored and equipped Bill to understand the real concerns behind the questions they asked. After sharing a few books, blogs, and some awkward role play, Bill started to get the hang of it.

Angie's conversations with Bill were a gift for more than just Bill. They eventually became a practical summer series for Upper Rooms nights on how to talk about Church teachings with non-Catholics. As more members of St. Mary's began to grow in their faith, they were beginning to share it. As they did, they inevitably encountered questions they were not equipped to answer. The summer series cemented the practical component of Upper Rooms. It met a real need of those who were setting out on mission, and it was bearing fruit. That fruit continued to be beautifully unexpected.

***

Bill almost fell out of his chair when two of the guys at work who had been asking some of the hardest questions announced they wanted to come with Bill to St. Mary's. His co-workers did not know it, but several people at St. Mary's were praying for them. Bill's co-workers came to Mass and then went to brunch with Bill, Lori, Paul, and Anna. The visit was fantastic.

On the way home, Bill was overwhelmed with gratitude not just for what the Lord had done in his co-workers' lives, but for how his own faith had grown as he learned how to share it in a way others could receive it. When Lori asked him why he was so quiet, Bill just smiled and wiped his eyes.

"I felt so frustrated when I couldn't answer their questions," he said. "But looking back, I would not do it differently. If I didn't have to learn the answers to their questions, I don't know that I would have grown in my faith the way I have."

The next month Bill gave a testimony at an Upper Rooms night of his experience learning how to share his faith with his co-workers. He told the story of their subsequent visit to St. Mary's. There were more than a few moist eyes as the group saw how their prayers and awkward practice sessions had made such a difference. Bill closed his testimony by saying, "I just want everyone at St. Mary's to learn how to share their faith like I did. It is the ultimate adventure to watch God work through you."

Bill's closing words echoed in Father Dave's heart. "I want everyone at St. Mary's to experience sharing their faith, too. Everyone seems to be too busy to share their faith. How are we going to do this?" he wondered. That question would linger in Father Dave's heart as they moved through the communication phase and finally began the process of alignment.

St. Mary's Alignment Phase

The alignment phase is all about unity and clarity. It unites all staff and volunteers around the ministries and processes that form your clear path. (See Chapter 10 beginning on page 141.)

Father Dave and the leadership team worked hard to communicate the clear path to the various ministry leaders in the parish. They listed all the ministry leaders. They also assigned each ministry a leadership team member to initiate an alignment conversation. It took several months, but the leadership team eventually reached every organization within the parish. As time passed, however, the scope of their communication quickly grew, moving them into the alignment phase.

Dawn was the first one to notice this shift from simple communication to alignment. She recognized a common pattern to almost every one of her visits. The greatest interest came as the conversation moved to the role a specific group might play in making disciples. Most of the ministries they visited would be described as "on-ramps." Those ministries were not part of the clear path, but they had the potential to connect people to ministries on the path. As the team worked with the ministry leaders, they discovered most of the ministries did not have any plan to connect their participants to the clear path. The good news was the ministry leaders were eager to help people connect and grow.

Dawn's background as a teacher came in handy as she took a crack at developing a worksheet. She wrote a brief background of the development of the parish's clear path. In simple but clear language, Dawn started with Jesus' commission to make disciples of all nations (Mt. 28:18ff) and how this mission has been passed to each person. She gently reminded people the souls of friends, family, neighbors, and co-workers were at stake.

She then provided a visual overlay of the thresholds and the ministries that were part of St. Mary's clear path. The worksheet's blank backside provided space to answer the following reflection questions.

- What step on our clear path does your ministry connect participants with?
- How many participants from your ministry have moved to their next step?
- What about your current mode of operation needs to change to support the parish's mission to make disciples?

Time to Pause

The leadership team was ready to schedule another round of visits to the ministries of the parish when Tom named the real problem.

"This is a great worksheet. I love the way it invites our ministry leaders into the conversation," he said, pausing before addressing a bigger issue.

"The problem is, we still have too much stuff happening around here. None of it is bad. It's just not connected. It's hard to see how things fit together because there are so many activities," he said.

Tom explained how he thought the new family faith formation would need more of Father Dave's time and energy. He also noted how long it took the leadership team to meet with all the various ministries and programs in the parish.

"This would be a lot easier if we didn't have so many ministries to align," Tom said, but immediately saw the concern on everyone's faces.

"I'm not saying we need to kill them off," he quickly added, "but maybe they could take a break while we get some of these new things established."

Tom went on to acknowledge how initially he had advocated being aggressive regarding how much they should do. He now was concerned they had too much on their plates and risked having their efforts to build a clear path swallowed by all the other activities in the parish.

The idea of asking certain ministries to pause their activity did not sit well with Father Dave. He suggested that all of them were necessary for people to find a place. Tom pointed out that finding an activity and finding a place to grow in faith were not the same thing. Father also objected because some ministries might not restart. Dawn told them pausing might be a good thing, since other new opportunities might help people grow faster. Finally, Father Dave confessed he just did not want to be the bad guy anymore. Between his rules for faith formation and the accusations of favoritism, he was a little wary about upsetting people again.

As the conversation unfolded, Angie tried to keep everyone focused on how they equipped their existing parishioners. She reminded everyone how relatively few parishioners at St. Mary's had been on the Awakening Retreat. "How are people supposed to invite others to the retreat if they have not experienced it themselves?" she asked.

Over several meetings, the team continued to wrestle with the challenge of so many ministries. They prayed together, discussed the situation, and prayed together again. Slowly but surely, they came back to two central convictions.

First, people cannot effectively invite others to come to a ministry on the clear path if they have not experienced it themselves.

Second, most leaders and participants had no margin to add anything more to their busy lives. The competition for people's attention and time would dissipate with a pause. It would also allow current leaders and parishioners to experience the clear path of discipleship for themselves.

The team developed a one-year plan to pause most existing ministries to make space for parishioners to experience the clear path ministries. They promoted a summer Awakening Retreat in a neighboring town to accommodate more parishioners during the pause year. They also increased the number of Grow Groups by inviting current group members to come to the small group training offered during Upper Rooms nights.

In the end, they decided to pause almost every ministry not on the clear path, except ministries for sacrament preparation.

Although it took Father Dave and the team a long time to come to this decision, they agreed when they did. They expected resistance and frustration, so they spent a significant amount of effort explaining why. They referred to the commission of Jesus to make disciples. They talked about how much progress had been made in developing the path. They explained how unfair it was to ask already busy people to simply do more. They also explained how hard it would be to invite others to something they had not experienced themselves.

Maybe it was the communications effort, or maybe it was just grace, but the resistance they had anticipated never materialized. Initially, there were more than a few skeptics, but the experience of the Awakening Retreat, the faith formation in Grow Groups and evangelization formation of the Upper Rooms quickly won them over.

People loved it. Parishioners had always thought of St. Mary's as a family. Although they had been acquaintances for years, many members did not really know one another. After sharing the Awakening Retreat, receiving faith formation in Grow Groups, and being equipped for mission in the Upper Rooms, they were becoming friends.

When the pause was over, the parish was far more united. Many parishioners began to get involved in the previously paused ministries because they received an invitation from a friend. The new ministries on the clear path were viewed as a source of unity rather than "favorites."

Time to Prune

During the pause year, the leadership team quickly realized that certain ministries should not resume. Several small fundraisers and the festival ended. Through prayer and discussion, it became clear that several of the faith formation options also needed to remain dormant. These programs were not bad, but they had become distractions. Most of the faith formation programs sincerely worked to follow Father Dave's rules and make their faith formation more engaging, but it did not work for some. Their design made it hard to meet anywhere except the parish center. They offered food and tried to introduce more prayer, but it was like trying to fit a square peg in a round hole.

Conversations about discontinuing most of the faith formation ministries went surprisingly well. These leaders felt an obligation to continue, but they themselves had grown weary with the task. There were a few tears, but the decision to end was a relief for almost everyone involved. Father Dave made it easier by showing them sincere gratitude and by honoring these ministries' fruitfulness at Upper Rooms nights.

Rather than quietly ending, leaders were publicly thanked and honored. They made it a celebration. Gifts were given and stories were told. It felt a little like a funeral wake, but in a good way. By ending well, Father Dave and the team created healthy closure. It eased the transition and seemed to prevent any resentments. A handful of those leaders even began to serve within new ministries.

The religious education program was a good example of a positive transition to new ministries. When St. Mary's offered both traditional classroom religious education and family faith formation, there was confusion and frustration. When Father and the team made the decision to end traditional classroom religious education, many of the classroom catechists retired. Others became traveling coaches for family faith formation by assisting parents who wanted help to better pass their faith to their children.

The Product of Pruning

After the pruning work concluded, Grow Groups remained the one adult faith formation step on St. Mary's clear path. These small groups had varied options for content, but the format was the same. Prayer, food, and community were always present. The clarity and simplicity created by this change had an immediate impact. The number of groups began to increase quickly. So did the faith of those who participated. The Grow Groups successfully provided a clear step for faith formation. They were flexible, accessible, and kept people connected.

The new family faith formation for religious education followed the same pattern. It mirrored the clear path for adults. Parents and their children attended a large group gathering once a month. Select moments of classroom instruction were reintroduced later. Most of the formation content, however, was delivered at home in family Grow Groups. These Grow Groups consisted of two or three families. Parents chose when to meet and then did the lessons together with their children.

There was some resistance, but the experience of family faith formation won people over. The kids and the adults enjoyed connecting with other families and really growing in their faith. Families were in sync spiritually. The clear path for children and parents was mutually reinforcing. Parents knew the path for their kids because they knew it for themselves, and vice versa. Most importantly, both children and parents felt St. Mary's was keeping their family together instead of providing multiple activities pulling them apart.

As the dust settled from the pruning work, Father Dave and the team experienced unique satisfaction. As they embraced clarity, the resistance they initially expected never materialized. It felt good to be clear and simple. They were starting to think it would be smooth sailing.

The Letter

A few weeks after the last spring Upper Rooms, Father Dave received a letter. It was Tuesday morning after his day off. The secretary handed it to him right after morning Mass, just as he walked into the office. It was not a letter of complaint. Father Dave knew how to respond to those. It was a letter from the bishop.

In his signature style, Bishop Samuels' letter was short and to the point. It was handwritten with some photocopies inside. "Dave, I have received a few letters from your parishioners," the letter said. "Some people are unhappy with what you are doing with the path thing. I am coming for a visit."

Bishop Samuels' letter to Father Dave included photocopies of two letters he had received. One was a complaint about the grounds crew helpers from a man Father Dave had never met. He was upset about all the time and energy being spent "on the new pathway when the current one was working just fine." Father wondered if the man was confused and talking about sidewalks.

The other one was a copy of a letter from Marge. Marge had been a key leader in the religious education program. Marge was an exceptional organizer and had kept St. Mary's program together for years. She had always seemed a little anxious, but she kept things running. Apparently, Marge was also a good record keeper because she had a long list of Father Dave's mistakes.

Reading the letter left Father Dave with a flood of emotions. He felt embarrassed. Nobody likes to have their "mistakes" listed for their boss. There was some truth in Marge's claim about Father Dave's changes in direction. The lack of clarity surrounding which faith formation programs would be part of the clear path affected Marge personally. *Her* classroom religious education program was initially highlighted before Father Dave and the team really embraced simplicity. Eventually it was one of the programs that was pruned.

He knew the decision to prune that ministry would be difficult for her, but he had no idea she was so upset. He felt angry because Marge did not come when they honored all who served in the religious education classroom program. She never said anything when the decision was made. As Father Dave reflected more, he decided he felt more betrayed than angry because she never even tried to talk to him.

Ultimately it saddened him because he hated to disappoint people, and he really hated the idea of Marge leaving the parish because she was upset about something he did. He consoled himself by thinking she would be happier at another parish and told the rest of the team at their regular meeting later that week.

"So, Marge is leaving the parish. She is apparently pretty upset with me. We should pray for her new pastor," Father Dave said. He thought the joke at the end would soften the blow. Most people reacted with surprise and disappointment, but they were not rattled. Tom's friend Diane had coached them to expect some resistance, so most of them took it in stride. Everyone seemed ready to move on until Angie spoke up.

"We don't need to pray for Marge's new pastor, we need to pray for Marge," Angie said. "She is not going to another parish. She has stopped going to church altogether."

The news hit like a ton of bricks. They were all a little stunned and confused. Instinctively, the team looked at Father

Dave. The silence lasted several moments. They could see some tears forming in Father Dave's eyes.

"This is exactly why we are trying to build a clear path," he said when he finally spoke. He stopped to take a long breath and steady his voice. "It's one thing for Marge to walk away from me or St. Mary's, but if she has stopped going to church, she is really walking away from Jesus. I take responsibility for whatever mistakes we made, but if she is walking away from Jesus because her program ended, that is exactly why we need a clear path. Our relationship with Jesus needs to mean more than a program or ministry."

Father Dave took another deep breath and then continued. "She also wrote a letter to Bishop Samuels complaining about how this path thing is ruining our parish," he added. A few eyebrows went up, but to Father Dave's relief the team held steady.

"Listen, I don't want to speak badly about Marge, but she was stuck," he said. "She faithfully served for many years, but I don't think she enjoyed it for quite some time. I don't think it was an overflow of her prayer. Maybe things could have been different if she had experienced the Awakening Retreat and some evangelization formation." The team nodded silently.

"You all know this stuff is hard for me, but honestly this just confirms why we need a clear path," Father Dave said.

"That's good," Tom said smiling gently. "Because we are going to need to figure out how to explain it to the bishop."

Bishop Samuels' Visit

The weeks leading up to Bishop Samuels' visit were rough for Father Dave and the team. They put on a brave face when they received the news, but the uncertainty and apprehension surrounding the bishop's visit was paralyzing. To be precise, their discouragement caused paralysis. They had worked so hard, and now they feared all their endeavors would be derailed due to critiques to which they had never been given a chance to personally respond.

Sometimes they felt confident they were doing the right thing. Other times they were not so sure. At the deepest level, they wondered if they had gone off track.

Father Dave would be the first to admit they were in uncharted territory. It seemed many Church leaders were talking about parish renewal, but most of the books they read were heavy on theory. Some clear best practices were emerging, and they tried to learn from others whenever they could. And although Father Dave and his team were sincere, they sometimes wondered if St. Mary's was doing it right.

The word had spread about the bishop's upcoming visit to address complaints he had received. Some of Father Dave's brother priests tried to comfort him by joking that maybe he was going to get "promoted" to chancery work. They meant well, but their expressions of support only highlighted the fact that St. Mary's was the only parish in the diocese moving in this direction. There were many good parishes in the diocese, but few were dynamic. Some parishes were growing, but only due to the real estate market. Whatever the reason, at least those other parishes were not shrinking.

St. Mary's was not continuing to shrink, but it was not growing yet either. Their Mass attendance had been in decline for decades, but their recent efforts seemed to slow this decline.

Hope could be found, however, in the growing number of people becoming Catholic at St. Mary's. This more than doubled from when Father Dave first arrived. There were many new faces at Mass, but total attendance was not consistently on the rise. Father Dave and the team felt sure they were on the cusp of a breakthrough. They could feel the momentum growing. They had spent so much time and energy building their clear path, but they did not have much to show for it in terms of numbers yet. They had stories of people whose lives were being changed, but they did not have the statistical evidence to prove they were on the right track.

The more Father Dave reflected, the more it became clear their approach was unique…and that would be hard to explain.

They were going to need to tell stories of what they had done and why they had done it. Maybe the stories could help the bishop feel the conviction that had inspired them and the momentum they were starting to sense.

***

Bishop Samuels had a no-nonsense reputation. He was kind and direct. He did not often intervene in parish matters. When he did, usually something was wrong. He knew most people experience the Church in their parishes. He had been a pastor and a seminary professor before being named a bishop. In meetings, he was often the last person to speak, but when he did, he spoke his mind. Whatever happened on the visit, Father Dave would know where things stood when it was over.

The fear and uncertainty surrounding the visit infected the whole team. Dawn addressed it first at the leadership meeting.

"It seems like we haven't really accomplished anything in weeks. Are we really in a holding pattern until the bishop comes?" she asked.

"It does feel like a holding pattern – we just keep circling the landing strip," Tom said.

"No," said Angie, "It feels like we lost power, and we're in a tailspin."

That brought them all a good laugh, and it helped give perspective. After some prayer and further discussion, the team decided the feedback from the bishop would be a good thing. They wanted to know if they were on the right track. Rather than minimize any of the work they had done, they decided to lean into it and tell the best story of what they had done and why.

Bishop Samuels' plan included celebrating Sunday Mass and staying for a brunch with Father Dave, the leadership team, and the pastoral council. The team agreed to ask someone to give a testimony followed by a formal presentation.

When the visit finally came, everyone was in surprisingly good spirits. The sense of dread had lifted when they named it.

In retrospect, their preparation for the visit had an encouraging effect. As they reviewed their work over the last few years, they were amazed by the progress. It all seemed so slow and ordinary day by day. As they stepped back and looked at the big picture, a sense of gratitude began to grow. They realized the Lord had done more than they had thought. The criticism had a way of erasing their memory, but their preparation for Bishop Samuels reminded them of all the Lord had done.

The best part of their preparation had been the discussion of who might share a testimony of their experience in St. Mary's clear path. They debated quite a bit on what was needed. As the conversation went on, people began to share names. There was a lot of passion, and everyone made a compelling case for why this person or that person would be the best.

Normally, these types of conversations drove Father Dave nuts. He had learned to tolerate healthy debate for the sake of good decision making, but it was not his natural disposition. Sensing the conversation could be wearing on Father Dave, the team paused to look at him. Father Dave was just sitting back and smiling.

"Do you realize, we can't seem to settle on who we want to share our story because we have so many people with amazing stories of God changing their lives? I wish the bishop could just hear this little debate," he said. The team realized that in trying to justify and tell the best story, they had listed the names of over two dozen people whose lives were changed by the ministries of the clear path.

Angie immediately thought of Bill and Paul. "Bill and Paul should share their story together," she said. Paul's eyes got big. Angie smiled and continued, "This thing is all about relationships, and the two of you play off each other really well."

"I like the idea of having men do it," added Tom. "Guys are usually lagging behind. If men are getting into their faith, something is really happening."

***

As usual, Bishop Samuels showed up a solid 30 minutes early for Mass. He liked to greet people on the way into Mass rather than after.

There was no hint of what he thought of the letters in the small talk before Mass. A bit of suspense hovered over brunch. Father Dave gave a brief welcome and introduction to Bill and Paul. They were nervous when they first started, but as they shared, they were clearly just two guys telling their story. It did not hurt that Bill showed some emotion as he talked about his experience on the Awakening Retreat and at Upper Rooms nights. Bill credited Paul and Angie for helping him connect. Paul pointed out it was really the whole community's efforts. Father Dave and the team were also moved as they listened to Bill and Paul retell their story together. It took all the discipline they had not to turn and stare at the bishop to see his reaction.

After Bill and Paul finished, Tom stood up to give a brief summary of their work on the clear path. Tom was a good presenter, but he was a little too thorough because he was nervous. He shared the mantra, "We are building a path to help people **connect, know, grow,** and **go** with Jesus." He was on slide 12 of 50 when the bishop kindly interrupted. Bishop Samuels had a charming sort of impatience about him. His leadership was marked by pragmatic realism.

"Tom," said Bishop Samuels. "I appreciate what you have prepared here, but I don't need the details. I can see you have a plan, and I can see that plan is working."

Tom was at a loss as to what to do next, so Father Dave spoke. "Thank you, Your Excellency," he began. "We have been at work on this for a few years, and we think it is working well. However, we wanted to show you everything we are doing, so you can tell us if we really are on the right track."

"Well, it's simple to me," the bishop said. "You have a plan to connect with people and to introduce them to Jesus. You know how to build them up and how to send them out. That is the whole point, isn't it?" Disbelieving heads nodded.

"Not everybody likes the way we're doing things," Angie said.

"If everybody did, you're probably not doing the right things," Bishop Samuels said with a wry smile. "Listen, Jesus and his mission were a sign of contradiction. His mission revealed hearts, and when you lean into his mission, you will reveal hearts, too." He paused and looked at everyone over his glasses that had slipped to the end of his nose. His slight smile reassured the team he had no concerns about the letters he had received.

"When Jesus describes his ministry, he talks about being the kind of shepherd that leaves the 99 in search of the one lost sheep," he continued. "You all are trying to do that. Those that are well do not need a physician."

"But it doesn't mean they don't think they deserve all your time," Father Dave said.

"Yes, I guess that is the hard part," said the bishop with a laugh. Bishop Samuels took a deep breath, removed his glasses, and briefly rubbed his eyes. Father Dave saw this mannerism enough to know whatever followed would be very direct.

"For years we bishops have been talking about evangelization. Most parishes that have tried to make it happen have centered their efforts on catechesis, good liturgy, and efficient administration. That stuff is all well and good, but it is for us, the insiders. The more I reflect on what is needed, the more I come back to this one question: Do we have a heart for lost sheep?" he said, slowly glancing around the room as he leaned forward in his chair.

"Our mission is to the fallen away and non-Christians, too. They are not outside of God's plan. We must ask ourselves, 'Who are they to Jesus, and who are they to us?'" he said, letting the words hang in the air for a moment before he sat back again.

"I don't just want you to do the same things we have always done faster and more efficiently. We must try some new approaches, and I am glad you are leading the way. Just do me one favor." Everyone nodded and leaned forward while Bishop Samuels put his hand on Father Dave's shoulder. "Don't let this guy work too hard. He is a good man, and you're lucky to have him. Priests don't grow on trees, so make sure he gets his rest."

Father Dave blushed and looked down. As Bishop Samuels looked around the room, he saw gratitude in their eyes. He smiled and stood up. He thanked everyone, quickly shook hands, and then he was gone.

St. Mary's Expansion Phase

The expansion phase is all about building a missing step on the clear path or expanding an existing step to make that ministry more fruitful. It is about building momentum and revisiting the clear path blueprint to see if any adjustments are necessary. (See Chapter 11 beginning on page 152.)

Bishop Samuels' visit had an energizing effect on Father Dave and the team. The next few months were extremely productive as they confidently worked at expanding their clear path.

To provide more focus, the team gathered for a two-day, offsite retreat at a cabin owned by one of the parishioners. Again, Diane played a key role in helping the team determine how to expand their evangelization formation. Diane led them through several visioning exercises with questions like: What do you want a missionary disciple in your parish to do? What does that look and sound like in real life? Much to Angie's embarrassment, the whole team turned and looked at her. They all wanted their leaders to do what Angie had done for Bill.

That offsite retreat led to the creation of an Upper Rooms team for evangelization formation headed by Angie. Angie invited Janice, Paul, and Bill to be on the team. Together they developed a proposal that included a rotation of topics for the Upper Rooms nights on prayer and mission. Each night would focus on one simple missionary skill. People would practice it for a month. The next Upper Rooms would begin with a short testimony of someone's experience sharing their faith.

The Upper Rooms team also proposed adding a retreat designed to introduce people to the person of the Holy Spirit. The weekend retreat, slated for the Easter season, would be designed to foster devotion to the Holy Spirit and introduce people more fully to the gifts, or charisms, the Spirit had given them for their personal mission of evangelization.

The retreat was an easy sell. People recognized the power of the Awakening Retreat. They also knew an additional retreat was needed. They noticed many people desired to repeat the Awakening Retreat simply because it had been such a profound moment of encounter. Repeating the Awakening experience really was not needed in their spiritual life, but no other retreat option was offered yet. The decision to offer a retreat focused on the Holy Spirit was a clear next step to expanding their evangelization formation. They called it the Upper Rooms Retreat.

The Upper Rooms Retreat stretched the comfort zone for some of St. Mary's parishioners. They knew about the Holy Spirit, but it was not the same as knowing him personally. The somewhat unpredictable style of the Holy Spirit could leave people a little uncomfortable. Most people were accustomed to a predictable experience of church. Additionally, some parishioners' prior experiences caused them to feel like second class citizens if they did not have certain spiritual gifts. These experiences were definitely *not* what Father Dave and the team wanted.

With the needs of St. Mary's parishioners in mind, they developed an outline for the retreat. There would be talks on God's love, the person of the Holy Spirit, and the specific gifts he gives disciples for mission. They built in two extended holy hours with Eucharistic adoration. The first holy hour was for healing and an experience of God's love. The second was to receive the gifts of the Spirit for evangelization and service. During each holy hour, prayer teams would walk around two by two to pray with individuals. Planning the schedule was the easy part.

They invited Father Ambrose to be the retreat master. He was a gifted teacher, and he knew the power of the Holy Spirit for evangelization. As a seminarian, Father Ambrose spent two years driving a van full of missionaries around Wisconsin and leading Confirmation retreats for middle and high school students. Father Ambrose was the perfect fit. His relaxed demeanor put people at ease.

The fruits from the Upper Rooms Retreat were too numerous to count, but two phenomena stood out. First, those attending the retreat seemed to always be in the right place. That is, they became especially effective connectors for people in key moments. The second phenomenon shared by retreatants was a new sense of confidence in their calling and mission. Wherever they served, they did so with more freedom, confidence, and awareness of how the Lord had uniquely gifted them.

Unexpected Overflow – Youth Ministry

The expansion of the clear path of discipleship at St. Mary's offered an additional surprise. The team responsible for coordinating the youth ministry had been watching the parish at large. The changes to religious education and family faith formation increased the number of young people interested in the youth group. The parish's young people had a real interest to grow in prayer and in how to share their faith.

Because so many of the parents and youth ministry team members heard Father Dave talk about the clear path, it was natural they would incorporate some of the ideas into the youth ministry program. They already had several opportunities for relational outreach built into the youth ministry program. At one point, it seemed all they did was relational outreach because they were trying to keep the few involved teens engaged. Now, however, these same teens were bringing their friends, and the relational outreach was serving as an invitation to young people whose families did not currently belong to St. Mary's.

The youth ministry leaders began to partner with another parish to attend an annual Encounter conference sponsored by a local college. That became the youth ministry's conversion moment. The conference was powerful and life-changing for the teens and the adult helpers. It was the perfect combination of a road trip, a retreat, and time spent with caring adults. The adults were definitely not "cool," but they clearly cared about the teens as people and not projects. The teens could tell.

Faith formation happened at the regular youth ministry nights. Leaders began to introduce the Grow Group model of small groups with food and relational prayer. The number of groups began to increase as teens who had experienced conversion at the college conference continued coming. Now they were hungry to learn and grow, and the momentum was contagious.

The most surprising development came when the teens in the youth group began attending the Upper Rooms nights. Young people, who had formerly felt awkward around adults, now found a source of wisdom they craved. Adults, who formerly only saw immaturity in the teens, were inspired by their sincere faith. Upper Rooms became a beautiful multigenerational event, and the Holy Spirit provided unity beyond age or family background.

The image on the next page shows St. Mary's clear path for both adults and youth. Notice how the clear path for youth mirrors the path for adults and converges in the Upper Rooms ministry.

A Clear Path of Discipleship

Thresholds of Conversion and Discipleship

  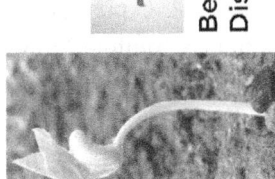  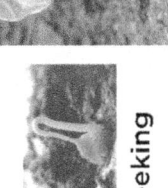 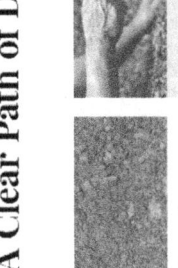 

Trust — Openness — Seeking — Decision — Beginning Disciple — Missionary Disciple — Fruitful Disciple

| Men's Softball | Awakening Retreat | Grow Groups | Upper Room Ministry |
| Youth BBQ Events | Encounter Conference | Youth Small Groups | |

The End of the Beginning

The building of a clear path of discipleship at St. Mary's was just the beginning of the parish's journey. As Father Dave and parish leaders looked back, they marveled at how the Lord led them on this journey. The fruit was undeniable. The parish was now visibly growing, and it was not due to the real estate market. The lives of their parishioners were being changed and the gospel was beginning to radiate out to the community at large. Both Catholic and non-Catholic churches noticed and started asking questions. The members of St. Mary's were really leaven in the wider community. Their teams still did not win much at softball, but they won where it really counted. They learned to make and mature disciples and to reach their little corner of the world with the Good News of Jesus Christ.

Questions for Reflection

1. Which characters in the case study do you identify with most and why?
2. How does your own story resemble Bill, Paul, Anna, or one of the others from the case study?
3. Who has served as a connector for you as you transitioned from one part of your journey to another?
4. How does your own story shape your desires to serve others?

Conclusion

The Challenge of Imagination

I believe the most urgent need for the Church in the United States today is pastoral conversion – a change in heart, mind, and habits back to our core missionary identity. I believe the Lord is calling us back to the most fundamental elements of our faith. It is hard to get more fundamental than the Great Commission. Jesus gives us one final command before he ascends into Heaven: "Go and make disciples" (Mt. 28:18ff).

The challenges to pastoral conversion in typical parish life are numerous. The call to make disciples is often not clear to leaders and other members of the community. The skills needed for this mission are sometimes beyond the experience and training of pastors and parish leaders. Distractions can overwhelm the desire to make and mature disciples as we drown in the responsibilities of maintaining institutions with diminishing resources. All these challenges are real, but the most significant challenge is surprisingly subtle.

Imagination is the most significant challenge. Praise God, the call to make disciples is becoming clearer, and the limits of our skills and experience can be overcome with the assistance of others. With a clear and compelling vision, we can fight through the distractions of our maintenance responsibilities. What stubbornly remains is the challenge to imagine what making disciples looks like in the community of faith we call a parish.

The concept of a clear path of discipleship is so helpful here because it takes making and maturing disciples from concept to concrete reality. Regardless of the programs and ministries included in that path, there is a process of conversion and discipleship which underlies these ministries. At the most foundational level, the Lord is calling individuals to himself, not just as disciples, but as missionary disciples he is sending to others.

This book attempts to stimulate the imagination for what making and maturing disciples using a clear path of discipleship can look like in a parish. Every parish has its own mission field. The history and people within a parish create unique and unrepeatable circumstances for the Lord to work. It is my hope this book provides you with a framework that leaves ample room for your creativity in partnership with the Holy Spirit.

Stepping Out in Faith

Many of us have become accustomed to simply managing decline, and that can be a full-time job. Shifting direction takes an enormous amount of energy, but there is hope and help as we step out in faith.

When we prioritize God's work, he comes to our aid. He is Lord of all, and he enters even the mundane details of administration and maintenance. From my experience, however, he only does so to the degree we prioritize making disciples. Counterintuitively, parishes that prioritize making disciples often have the most efficient administration and effective maintenance. The Lord labors with and for us when we give our best to the primary mission, making disciples.

It is a trap to think that we can begin the task of evangelization only after we have everything in order. The daily duties of maintenance and ordinary pastoral care are often overwhelming. To prioritize making disciples requires faith. Sometimes it takes heroic faith to look beyond the leaking roof and the cracks in the parking lot to address the foundation of a parish. And by foundation, I am not referring to the facility's foundation, but the foundational commission given by Jesus to make disciples. It is precisely in the prioritization of making disciples that we will find the supernatural assistance needed for everything required of us – both mission and maintenance alike.

My invitation is to step out in faith. Begin building a clear path of discipleship in your parish and watch the Lord come to your aid. May God bless and reward you for your efforts.

Appendix I: Thresholds of Conversion and Discipleship

Thresholds of Conversion and Discipleship

Trust

A person has a positive association with Jesus or an individual Catholic and may begin asking questions out of passive curiosity.

Openness

A person admits to a general need or desire for personal spiritual change. This is not the same as a commitment to specific changes.

Seeking

A person moves from being passive to actively seeking to know the God who is calling him or her. The seeker is engaged in a spiritual quest.

Decision

The decision, in faith, to follow Jesus as an obedient disciple in the midst of the Church, which brings about new life.

Beginning Disciple

A person has committed to following Jesus by turning away from sin, and makes any sacrifice in order to personally grow, and lives habits of the Christian life.

Missionary Disciple

A person has decided to personally answer the call to take part in the mission of the Church by sharing the Good News.

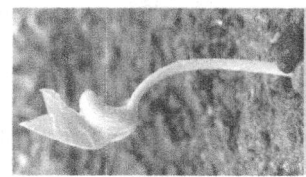

Fruitful Disciple

A person is fully equipped for lifelong Catholic mission and makes any sacrifice to help another person to grow spiritually.

Appendix II: Steps on a Clear Path of Discipleship

A Clear Path of Discipleship | Thresholds of Conversion and Discipleship

Trust	Openness	Seeking	Decision	Beginning Disciple	Missionary Disciple	Fruitful Disciple

A person has a positive association with Jesus or an individual Catholic and may begin asking questions out of passive curiosity.	A person admits to a general need or desire for personal spiritual change. This is not the same as a commitment to specific changes.	A person moves from being passive to actively seeking to know the God who is calling him or her. The seeker is engaged in a spiritual quest.	The decision, in faith, to follow Jesus as an obedient disciple in the midst of the Church, which brings about new life.	A person has committed to following Jesus by turning away from sin, and makes any sacrifice in order to personally grow, and lives habits of the Christian life.	A person has decided to personally answer the call to take part in the mission of the Church by sharing the Good News.	A person is fully equipped for lifelong Catholic mission and makes any sacrifice to help another person to grow spiritually.

Relational Outreach	Conversion Moment	Faith Formation	Evangelization Formation

Appendix III
Discernment Rosary
Facilitator's Guide

The Vision for a Discernment Rosary:

We are anchoring ourselves in the prayer of the Rosary. We will take time before each decade's prayers to ask God a specific question. We will pause for a minute or two in silence to listen to him. Then, everyone will have an opportunity to share the thoughts, feelings, and desires that come to them in prayer. The convergence of what is shared helps the group to discern what God is saying.

Leaders should listen for 1. common themes, 2. comments that bring peace and consolation, and 3. consistent words and images.

PRAYING THE DISCERNMENT ROSARY:

1. Begin with the Apostles' Creed, Our Father, three Hail Marys, and a Glory Be.
2. Before each decade: Ask the Lord a discernment question, such as: *"Who have you provided to lead this ministry?"*
3. Say an Our Father, ten Hail Marys, and a Glory Be.
4. At the end of the decade, repeat the discernment question used at the beginning of the decade. Pray aloud: Lord, is there anything you want to say to us?
5. Ask the group to listen for a few minutes for God's response.
6. After a minute or two of silence, ask the group to share anything they may have received.
7. Write down the comments shared and watch for common themes.
8. Feel free to pray as many decades as needed depending on time available.

Reminders: We are not asking the Lord to confirm our ideas, but to hear his ideas. We want to enter the process with humility and ask God to show us what he wants. If you do not know which question to ask, simply ask what he wants you to know. When you listen, do not try to figure it out. Just listen.

Appendix IV

Discernment Rosary
Sample Questions

1. Lord, where are you already at work making disciples in our parish?

2. Where would you like us to start building first?

3. Who have you provided as leaders for the new initiatives?

4. What do you want to say to us as a group?

5. What pitfalls should we be careful to avoid?

6. Disciples in our parish are or look like…?

7. People become mature disciples in our parish by…?

8. The ministries that coincide with our process are…?

Appendix V
Methods of Relational Prayer

Relational prayer is simply a form of personal prayer, which emphasizes the fact that God, the Lord of the universe, has chosen to be in relationship with us. He calls us friends (Jn. 15:15) and wants to do what friends do. He wants to talk.

Conversation with God is nothing new in Catholic prayer tradition. It is at the heart of the teachings of great spiritual masters, such as Saint Teresa of Avila, Saint John of the Cross, and Saint Benedict. What I offer here is a simple synthesis of some characteristics of relational prayer and a few methods, associated with the Institute for Priestly Formation, that I have personally found effective in teaching relational prayer to others.[29]

Characteristics of Relational Prayer

Whole books could be written on the characteristics of relational prayer. I will highlight three that I think describe its unique qualities for making missionary disciples.

Personal – Relational prayer is a personal form of prayer. It is about relating *your* thoughts, feelings, and desires to the Lord. It is usually not part of communal liturgical prayer like the Mass. It is typically not devotional like the Rosary or Chaplet of Divine Mercy. Although personal prayer is distinct from liturgical prayers and devotions, they are mutually beneficial. The habit of personal prayer enriches liturgical and devotional prayer, and they often help inform and inspire personal prayer.

Honest – Above all, relational prayer must be honest. It must be relating what we are really thinking and feeling to the

---

[29] I am particularly indebted to the Institute for Priestly Formation (IPF) in Omaha, Nebraska. The work and resources of IPF continue to be a blessing to seminarians, priests, bishops, and countless lay men and women across the country. You can learn about IPF online at priestlyformation.org.

Lord – authentically. He already knows if we are angry. He cares and wants an honest relationship. The prayer of the saints and the great men and women of scripture is sometimes surprisingly honest. Don't be afraid to imitate them.

Consistent – Relational prayer must be consistent to be fruitful. This typically looks like daily quiet time set aside for prayer. Prayer tends to happen more consistently when you have a plan. People who are consistent in prayer generally know when and where they will pray each day. They also know *how* they will pray when that time comes. They have a method for prayer.

Methods of Relational Prayer

ARRR

ARRR is a simple acronym, developed by the Institute for Priestly Formation, for remembering the fundamental dynamics of prayer. Technically, it is not a method as much as it is a way of recognizing what is happening in our hearts and minds, regardless of the method of prayer. All forms of prayer include these dynamics. Knowing them can help make personal prayer more fruitful.

Acknowledge – Begin by acknowledging the thoughts, feelings, and desires of our hearts. This can be a challenge since so much of our world is designed to distract us from noticing anything beneath the surface. Honest prayer begins with acknowledging how we are feeling and thinking.

Relate – Next, we relate what is going on in our hearts and minds to the Lord. Just talk to him. Have faith. Just like a friend, he cares and wants to know.

Receive – Similar to other conversations, we must take time to actively listen. The Lord will offer us something in answer to what we have related to him. His answer may be peace. It might be a memory offering insight. It might be a scripture verse leading to clarity or suggesting action. It might not be what you expect, but it will be something good.

Respond – After receiving what the Lord offered, we need to respond. This may be a simple expression of gratitude or a resolution to new action. It might be a further development of the conversation.

WRAP

WRAP is another acronym for prayer and a method for Lectio Divina from the book, *WRAP Yourself in Scripture,* by Karen and Lawrence Dwyer, published by the Institute for Priestly Formation. It combines the traditional steps of Lectio Divina with journaling.[30] Lectio Divina is Latin for divine reading. It is an ancient method of prayer rooted in the slow and prayerful reading of scripture. I find WRAP especially helpful for two simple reasons. First, the acronym is easier to remember than the traditional Latin terminology. Secondly, I find the combination of reading with journaling fights distraction and draws me deeper into conversation with the Lord.

Write – The first step after reading a few verses of scripture is to write the verse or the image that comes to your mind. *I noticed how calm the water seems as Jesus preaches from the boat.*

Reflect – Read the verses again and reflect on what caught your attention. Turn it over in your mind and notice what is happening in the scene or verses you have chosen. Write out your reflection. *Jesus' words are not necessarily easy to accept, but they come from his love for us.*

Apply – Read the passage a third time and begin to apply what you are noticing. Where are you in the story? What lesson is the Lord teaching you? Record the application you found in

---

[30] From *WRAP Yourself in Scripture* by Karen and Lawrence Dwyer, 2011, 2018, Institute for Priestly Formation. © *2011, 2018* by Karen and Lawrence Dwyer. Adapted with permission. It can be found online at priestlyformation.org/resources/ipf-publications.html

your journal. *Jesus' words calm my heart even when they are challenging.*

Prayer – Read the verses one more time. This time respond back in prayer. Write your simple, honest, heartfelt prayer, and take a few moments to just rest in Jesus' love. *Lord, calm my heart and help me to accept your word to me as a gift of your love.*

The Holy Spirit is both the author of prayer and the driver behind our evangelization efforts. Personal relational prayer is key to discerning where the Lord is leading. It is the foundation to courageous invitation and the patient accompaniment that brings a clear path to life. A clear path provides the framework. Our efforts to mature disciples in the habits of relational prayer are a big part of what makes the framework fruitful. For more on forming disciples in prayer check out the writing of Father Scott Traynor, *The Parish as a School of Prayer: Foundations for the New Evangelization*, Institute for Priestly Formation, 2013.

Appendix VI:
Clear Objectives
Facilitator's Guide

Framing the Vision

The purpose of this exercise is to support the pastor in building a clear path of discipleship.

This is a process for setting and *achieving* goals to move the parish forward.

Step 1: Start Brainstorming Priority Objectives
- Have people brainstorm individually on the Clear Objectives Worksheet (Appendix VII).
- Share and discuss as a group.
- Facilitator, look for pitfalls in the brainstorming process (see below).

Step 2: The Group Picks One Priority
- Groups will often list three or four priorities.
- As a group, select one priority to get started.
  Pro Tip: In the beginning, the group should choose only one priority they can achieve within three months.

Step 3: Define the Win and Begin the Planning Guide
- Begin visualizing the "win." What does success look like for this priority? Where are things right now? What are the obstacles?
- Begin filling out the Planning Guide (Appendix VIII).

Optional: Repeat for one or two additional priorities.

Potential Pitfalls to Avoid

Maintenance Priorities – Gently determine if all the priorities are focused on maintenance. Maintenance may be necessary immediately, but the goal is to get past urgent maintenance needs as soon as possible to pursue the mission to make disciples.

Too Many Priorities – Trying to pursue everything at once is overwhelming and unrealistic. Any more than two or three priorities will likely cause frustration and fail.

Invisible Priorities – Some things are important priorities but are not acknowledged. Fish for any unspoken priorities like hiring and training.

Rigidity – Do not be ashamed to adjust priorities if circumstances warrant.

Forgetting to Celebrate – Encourage the group to offer praise to the Lord and to celebrate even small wins together.

Appendix VII
Clear Objectives Worksheet

Step 1: Write down one or two potential objectives:
If we do nothing else in the next three months, we must:

Step 2: Pick one priority objective as a team:

Step 3: Define the win:

What does success look like?

Where are we currently?

What obstacles are in the way?

Appendix VIII

Planning Guide

In the next three months, we absolutely must:

Priority: _____

Milestones:	Action Steps:	Point Person:	Due Date:	Measurement:

Appendix IX: St. Mary's Highway to Heaven

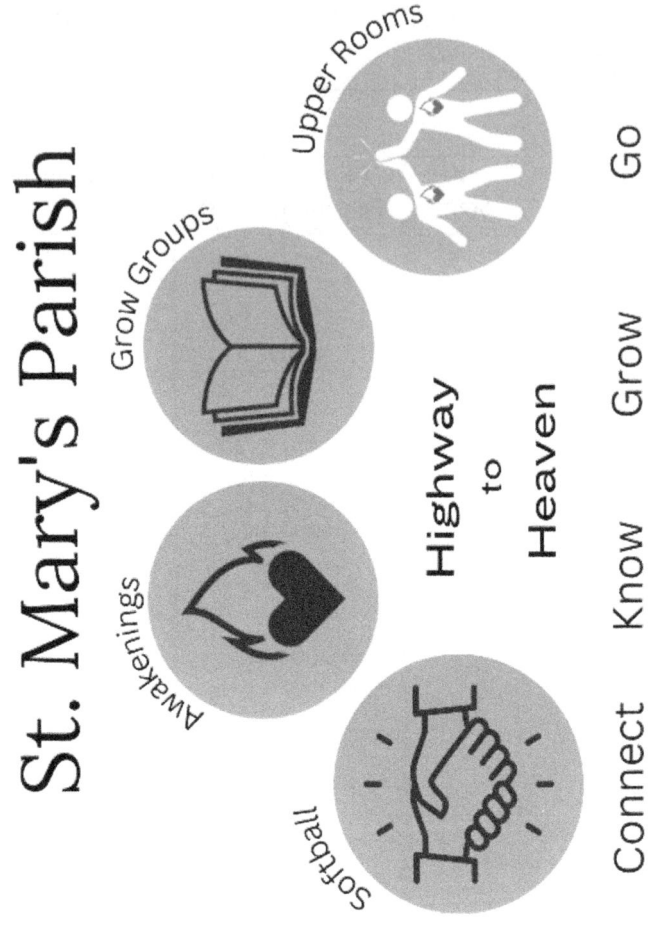

Made in the USA
Monee, IL
08 December 2023

48615666R10131